William Shakespeare: Comedies, Histories, and Tragedies
Part III

Professor Peter Saccio

THE TEACHING COMPANY ®

PUBLISHED BY:

THE TEACHING COMPANY
4151 Lafayette Center Drive, Suite 100
Chantilly, Virginia 20151-1232
1-800-TEACH-12
Fax—703-378-3819
www.teach12.com

ISBN 1-56585-639-2

Peter Saccio, Ph.D.

Leon D. Black Professor of Shakespearean Studies
Dartmouth College

Peter Saccio has taught at Dartmouth College since 1966. He chaired the English department from 1984 to 1988; in addition, he has won Dartmouth's J. Kenneth Huntington Memorial Award for Outstanding Teaching. He has served as visiting professor at Wesleyan University and at University College in London.

He received a B.A. from Yale University and a Ph.D. from Princeton. He is the author of *The Court Comedies of John Lyly* (1969) and *Shakespeare's English Kings* (1977), the latter a classic in its field. He edited Middleton's comedy *A Mad World, My Masters* for the Oxford *Complete Works of Thomas Middleton* (1996). He has published or delivered at conferences more than twenty papers on Shakespeare and other dramatists.

Professor Saccio has directed productions of *Twelfth Night*, *Macbeth*, and *Cymbeline*. He has devised and directed several programs of scenes from Shakespeare and from modern British drama, and he served as dramaturg for the productions of his Dartmouth colleagues. He has acted the Shakespearean roles of Casca, Angelo, Bassanio, and Henry IV as well as various parts in the ancient plays of Plautus and the modern plays of Harold Pinter, Tom Stoppard, and Peter Shaffer.

Table of Contents

William Shakespeare: Comedies, Histories, and Tragedies
Part III

William Shakespeare:
Comedies, Histories, and Tragedies

Scope:

In 36 half-hour lectures, *William Shakespeare: Comedies, Histories, and Tragedies* introduces the plays of Shakespeare and delineates the achievement that makes Shakespeare the leading playwright in Western civilization. The key to that achievement is his "abundance," not only the number of plays he wrote and the length of each one, but also the variety of human experiences they depict, the multitude of actions and characters they contain, the combination of public and private life they deal with, the richness of feelings they express and can provoke in an audience and in readers, and the fullness of language and suggestion.

The first two lectures are introductory. They consider how Shakespeare's plays have been found valuable by four centuries of readers, and how they have been interpreted and reinterpreted by the generations who have read and seen them. The lectures consider the kind of theater for which he wrote, the characteristic structures of his plays, and the way the plays easily mingle events from different realms: different social levels, different levels of realism, different metaphysical contexts.

The course then proceeds to consider the plays in terms of genre. Lectures Three through 10 discuss four comedies. *Twelfth Night* offers an example of basic Shakespearean comic structure and subject matter: courtship by several young couples. Renaissance courtship practices are discussed, together with their implications about the place of romantic love in human life as a whole. Shakespeare also includes in his survey of lovers Malvolio the ambitious steward, for whom courtship is a means of social advancement. *The Taming of the Shrew* provides a more realistic look at bourgeois marriage customs and the place of a strong woman in a patriarchal society. It shows as well Shakespeare experimenting with an unusually sharp collision of romance and farce. *The Merchant of Venice* entails a particularly lofty form of romantic idealism in the courtship plot, but it confronts that idealism with the problematic, possibly tragic, character of Shylock, who has forced generations of actors into reinterpretation of Shakespeare. *Measure for Measure* shows Shakespeare on the verge of breaking out of comic conventions altogether. The characters marry at the end, as is customary, but the route to their unions is a gritty path entailing near-rape and near-execution via the courtrooms and the sexual underground of a corrupt modern society.

Lectures 11 through 18 deal with five plays drawn from English history. The nature of the history play is explained. Richard III is followed through the arc of his villainous and entertaining career. *Richard II* raises constitutional problems that vex us still: what can be done with a ruler who is undoubtedly entitled to rule and is also damaging the realm? The two plays named after Henry IV show Shakespeare's widest scope in depicting the realm of England from throne room to tavern to countryside, and they introduce Shakespeare's most remarkable comic creation, Falstaff. In *Henry V*, Shakespeare kills Falstaff in a scene of extraordinary artistic skill and emotional effect, and then takes the king to a military victory that still arouses all our conflicted convictions about the morality of warfare.

Lectures 19 through 36 deal with Shakespeare's tragedies. They show him taking Romeo and Juliet, who should be the leading pair of lovers in a comedy, and plunging their private bliss in the public violence of a city torn by feud. Why ancient Rome was important to Shakespeare (and to the Renaissance as a whole) is explored in two lectures on *Julius Caesar*. Two lectures on *Troilus and Cressida* show Shakespeare re-writing Homer into a bitter satire on vainglorious men and unfaithful women. Finally, three lectures apiece are devoted to each of the four greatest tragedies, *Hamlet*, *Othello*, *King Lear*, and *Macbeth*, so that the richness and variety of each can be explored. Emphasis falls on the scope of the tragic effect: Shakespeare's acute development of the inner consciousness in his tragic soliloquies, placed within the far-ranging philosophical and theological implications of tragic events for the whole of human life.

As with his students at Dartmouth, Professor Saccio expects his listeners and viewers to have some familiarity with the plays (he does not waste time on basic plot summary), but otherwise he provides the critical tools necessary for the appreciation of Shakespeare's world, his artistry, his significance, and his emotional power.

Lecture Twenty-Five
Hamlet: The Abundance of the Play

Scope:

This lecture begins by considering the classic status of *Hamlet*, locating that quality in its combination of familiarity and strangeness. This quality of being an "old thing made new" is sustained by the range of characters and actions, the variety of traits within the leading personage, and especially in the placement of events so that developments surprise the audience.

The lecture then explores what has been called the interrogative nature of the play, how it calls up "thoughts beyond the reaches of our souls," inquiring into the nature of death and the veracity of ghosts.

Outline

I. It is the mark of a classic that it always seems both new and old. Shakespeare's *Hamlet* seemed new and old even when it first appeared in 1600.

   A. The earliest written version of the story was by the monk Saxo Grammaticus about 1200. It appears in French in François de Belleforest's *Histoires Tragiques* in 1570 and reached the Elizabethan stage in the late 1580s in a play now lost, referred to by scholars as the "Ur-Hamlet," probably written by Thomas Kyd. Contemporary references to this play are derisory.

   B. Shakespeare's version is his longest play (nearly 4,000 lines) with his longest leading role. It is so full of material that even those who know it may be surprised by some of its contents when reading or seeing it again.

      1. It contains characters of all sorts: kings, courtiers, pirates, players, gravediggers, a ghost, and many others.

      2. The action ranges from a formal court council to a scene in which two young men jump into the grave of a suicidal madwoman.

      3. The title character is a prince, a son, a nephew, a lover, a poet, a swordsman, a near-suicide, a student of philosophy, a critic of the theatre.

II. The material of the play is often deliberately placed so as to surprise the audience.

    A. The first appearance of the ghost interrupts what had seemed to be a speech of sustained exposition. The visual effect overtakes the narrative.

    B. When Hamlet first sees the ghost, the same kind of ambush is arranged, but with greater impact and significance.

        1. A fourteen-line academic discourse on *hamartia* is interrupted by the ghost's appearance.

        2. The ghost is undeniable, but ambiguous.

        3. The unexpected event overtakes theory.

        4. Hamlet shifts from exposition to prayer.

    C. Scenes are arranged so that the focus of the audience is split (as noted by the critic Maynard Mack).

        1. The second scene of the play is an example of this.

        2. Do we look at Claudius, or at Hamlet, off to the side?

III. Much of the play takes place in the interrogative mood: people frequently ask questions, from the opening "Who's there?" to the famous "To be or not to be: that is the question."

    A. The play questions facts and raises mysteries.

    B. The questioning reaches its highest pitch with the appearance of the ghost in Act I.

    C. Tragedies regularly end in death, but this tragedy questions what it is like to *be* dead.

        1. C. S. Lewis proposed that death could well be the subject of this play.

        2. In *Hamlet*, being *after* death is a central feature.

IV. The ghost exemplifies the mysterious qualities of the play.

    A. Catholic writers of the 16th century suggested that ghosts came from Purgatory with legitimate requests to make of living people.

    B. Protestant writers suggested that ghosts were demons seeking to draw the people to whom they appeared into damnation.

    C. Skeptics suggested that ghosts were hallucinations produced by unsound minds.

    D. Shakespeare uses all three theories without privileging one.

1. The ghost describes its condition in mostly Catholic terms.
2. Hamlet contemplates the possibility that the ghost is a devil (the Protestant theory).
3. Horatio tends to think of it as a hallucination, as does Gertrude.
4. Shakespeare uses this ghost to give Hamlet a problem and to give us the experience of encountering a ghost, thus forcing us into the same position as Hamlet.
5. This ghost is real, ambiguous—and dangerous.

Essential Reading:

Shakespeare, *Hamlet*.

Supplementary Reading/Viewing:

See *Hamlet* in BBC video (with Derek Jacobi) or one of the films starring, respectively, Laurence Olivier, Mel Gibson, Kenneth Branagh.

Booth, "On the Value of *Hamlet*."

Mack, "The World of Hamlet."

Wilson, *What Happens in* Hamlet.

Questions to Consider:

1. Do you agree with C. S. Lewis that the subject of Hamlet could well be death? Count the number of deaths and consider both the ways these characters died and the reactions of the remaining characters to these deaths. What insights does this exercise yield?

2. How effective is the ghost in startling 20th-century viewers, as compared to those in Shakespeare's time? If your answer is "very effective," why do you say so? If your answer is "not very effective," suggest another way for Hamlet to be roused to action early in the play.

Lecture Twenty-Five—Transcript
Hamlet: The Abundance of the Play

Hamlet is always old and always new. Any classic is; it is the mark of a classic that it is old, that many people have read it or seen it, enjoyed it and been enlightened by it. It has stood the test of time. It is also new; people are always rereading it, rediscovering it, reenacting it, finding that it offers new things to them, finding things in it that they had forgotten were there. A favorite line for me in the play just now is, "Thoughts beyond the reaches of our souls." It's one of Hamlet's lines when he's first confronting the ghost. I ran across it quoted in an essay on Hamlet, and thought I've never really thought about that line before, and what a marvelous and paradoxical line it is: "Thoughts beyond the reaches of our souls," thoughts that we can't actually think. I had to go back to the text and check that it really was there, in Act I, Scene IV.

Shakespeare's *Hamlet* was always old and always new, even in 1600. In the opening scene of the play, we are introduced to Horatio, an alert, skeptical college classmate of Hamlet's who has been drawn out at midnight because he has refused to believe that something supernatural is happening on the battlements of Elsinore. His skepticism is marked in his first full line, "What, has this thing appear'd again to-night?" Oddly enough, that question may have verbalized some reservations felt by the original audience of *Hamlet* at the Globe Theatre in the year 1600. They might reasonably have asked, "What, has this thing appeared again this afternoon?" he story of Hamlet was at least four centuries old by the time that Shakespeare got hold of it. It had been first written fully down by a monk called Saxo Grammaticus,in *A History of the Danes*—Saxo Grammaticus, "the Saxon who could write," very rare in the year 1200, apparently. It was taken up in French in the sixteenth century by a man named Belleforest in 1570.

Then, in the 1580s, there was a stage version in the Elizabethan theater, a play that we refer to now as the "Ur-Hamlet," probably written by Thomas Kyd, but it's a play that is now lost. It may never have been put into print, but it certainly was played in the late 1580s and through the 1590s. It was also sneered at. All the surviving references to the "Ur-Hamlet" are derogatory. The passage from Thomas Nashe, from which we deduce that Kyd wrote it, implies that it was a slapdash piece of formula work. Nashe writes, "If you entreat him fair, on a frosty morning, he will provide you whole Hamlets—I mean whole handfuls, of tragical speeches." Another Elizabethan mentions the voice of the ghost in this early Hamlet play, "The ghost which cried so miserably in the theater, like an oyster wife, Hamlet, revenge." Like an oyster wife? "Cockles, mussels; Hamlet, revenge." Hardly the sort of thing that would harrow us with fear and wonder.

The earlier ghosts of the Elizabethan stage provided Shakespeare's audience with very little preparation for what Shakespeare gives them in his ghost, what he calls "the majesty of buried Denmark," a ghost that is ominously silent for his first three appearances onstage, and is sufficiently impressive, without speaking and without shrieking, to reduce a skeptical Stoic like Horatio to fear and wonder. This thing is there, but it is also new. It has a new power, a new intensity.

One of the new things about the play is its scale. It is Shakespeare's longest play, nearly 4000 lines long, almost twice the length of *Macbeth*. An uncut performance takes somewhere between four and five hours; I've seen that, twice. The prince himself is, by far, Shakespeare's longest leading part. He's on stage for a tremendous stretch of time, particularly in the middle of the play. There is so much in it that even Shakespearean scholars may forget where a particular speech comes, or the exact sequence of episodes. I've been reading student papers on Hamlet for many years, but students still point out things to me that I hadn't thought of, that I hadn't realized.

The play is large, not only in its scale, but in its range. There is a large range of characters; there is a king, of course, and a royal family, and the prime minister, Polonius, and his family. There are other lords and courtiers, and there are university students, and there are traveling players, and there are gravediggers, soldiers, and ambassadors, a priest, and a ghost. The range of action is very wide: a formal court council scene; rehearsing and putting on a play; soliloquizing; telling Mother to shape up her sex life; digging a grave; burying a suicidal madwoman, and jumping in and out of the grave of that suicidal madwoman; fighting a duel at length, with many passes; and killing some of the bystanders, who happen to include the King and Queen of Denmark.

The facets of the hero's character are abundant as well. Hamlet is a prince, of course. He is also a son; a nephew, which makes him a stepson to the same man; he's a lover; he's a poet; he's a swordsman, a near suicide, a philosophy student, and a theater critic. That's why Hamlet is such a great test role. Any ambitious actor, any actor with classical ambitions, has got to play this part to test himself against it. Can he encompass all that variety and abundance in a coherent performance? You're a serious actor; you've got to have Hamlet on your resume somewhere.

In 1600, when it first came out, and now, the play is newly powerful and intense—not only because of the scale and the range of the action, but also because of its rhythm, its sequence, its presentation as a theatrical piece. If we want to see this thing again tonight, and again in many productions over a lifetime, it is because the thing is alive. Its rhythms and its constructions give us the obliquity, the solidity, and the occasional odd clarities that we recognize as the real thing, life felt along the pulse. They give us, visually and hourly, the impression of genuine selves going through disturbing experience. The distinctive mark, I think, of this genuineness, this intensity and aliveness, is that it overtakes us, it ambushes us, and it provides the shock of recognition. The habitual expectations of reasonable people are redirected, are countered, are ambushed by fresh events, fresh facts. Both the old pattern and the new development are rendered solidly enough so that the reasonable people must struggle to accommodate both in the same act of apprehension. We in the audience must struggle likewise.

It is by such overtaking in rhythm that the ghost of Hamlet's father is first introduced into the play. The play opens with a tense series of challenges in the cold darkness of the battlements of Elsinore, and then that tenseness is salted by the skepticism of Horatio. Then that gives way to what apparently is going to be a piece of ordinary exposition. Nothing is really happening at the moment on the battlements, so Horatio suggests that they all sit down. Specifically, he invites Bernardo to give a full account of the previous night's events. To the audience that doesn't know the story, or even to one who does but has forgotten the exact sequence of incidents, it would appear that we're about to hear a narrative about the ghost, and Bernardo begins in appropriate fashion:

> Last night of all,
>
> When yond same star that's westward from the pole
>
> Had made his course to illume that part of heaven

> Where now it burns, Marcellus and myself,
>
> The bell then beating one—

I just read five lines. The narrative is very leisurely; the syntax is suspended with numerous subordinate clauses. We're apparently in for a long story, but while this five-line sentence of iambic pentameter is gracefully unreeling itself, without yet having attained to the energy and dignity of a main verb, "enter Ghost." The ghost becomes the verb. The ghost exerts Bernardo's elegant syntax, displacing the narrative with fresh event. A visual effect overtakes the narrative line. That's a small example.

When Hamlet himself first sees the ghost three scenes later, the pattern of overtaking is developed with much greater impact and significance. Hamlet's first sighting of the ghost is a moment very famous in theatrical history. Actors from the seventeenth century to the twentieth have been minutely discussed, praised, or damned for the way they handled the first sighting of the ghost, Hamlet's start of astonishment. Frequently, they have been painted, photographed, etched or woodcut in that posture. The most famous example is in the eighteenth century, David Garrick, the greatest Shakespearean actor of the English eighteenth century.

Garrick's Hamlet had been strolling upstage with his back to the audience, when Horatio suddenly calls to him, "Look, my lord, it comes!" Garrick was wearing a full-length black cloak—of course, he's entirely dressed in black—a large black hat, sword and so forth. He's going upstage, Horatio cries out, and he whirled around, this hand knocking off the hat; the cloak, of course, swung wide with the energy; the other hand extended at a lower level than the right hand; and his whole body leaning forward with a start of an astonishment at such an angle that the other actors onstage had to support him. He could not stand up by himself. It was an extravagant moment, as eagerly awaited at the Drury Lane Theatre as a prima donna's high C is nowadays in an opera house. It could be as savagely criticized as a high C in an opera house, when the soprano cracks on the note. Boswell asked Dr. Johnson, "Would not you, sir, start as Mr. Garrick does if you saw a ghost?" and Johnson replied, "I hope not, sir. If I did, it would frighten the ghost." I have no objections to a fine tableau, but theater is not statuary; it does not exist in just one frozen pose. It is a temporal art. *Hamlet* exists in time, and the intensity and power for conviction in that passage lies in its pacing, not just the momentary pose that he strikes.

The start of astonishment occurs after Hamlet has spent some 30 lines discussing the low Danish habit of drinking to excess: "The King doth wake to-night and keep his rouse." Hamlet discusses the King's drinking in a characteristically intellectual fashion. In a sentence that's 14 lines long with fearfully convoluted grammar, he generalizes, from Denmark's reputation for drunkenness, to the fatal effect upon anyone of a single flaw of whatever kind. It goes like this:

> So oft it chances in particular men
>
> That, for some vicious mole of nature in them,
>
> As, in their birth—wherein they are not guilty,
>
> Since nature cannot choose his origin—
>
> Or by the o'ergrowth of some complexion,
>
> Oft breaking down the pales and forts of reason,
>
> Or by some habit that too much o'erleavens
>
> The form of plausive manners, that these men
>
> I say, carrying the stamp of one defect,
>
> Being nature's livery, or fortune's star,—
>
> Their virtues else—be they as pure as grace,
>
> As infinite as man may undergo—
>
> Shall in the general censure take corruption
>
> From that particular flaw.

His discussion of Claudius' drinking habits leads him, in fact, to a very academic exposition of Aristotle's theory of *hamartia*, the tragic fault that undermines the hero of a play. It's a very long speech, followed by the whirling movement, and then Hamlet says, "Angels and ministers of grace defend us!" It is that sort of break in a concerted piece of rhythm, going over a number of minutes, that makes the play seem so solid, so vivid to me. Our theorizing about the causes of human affairs often is derailed by stark fact, especially if the facts are both undeniable and ambiguous, and the ghost *is* undeniable and ambiguous. Hamlet and Horatio, like the good university students they are, pass the time of waiting by discussing some ideas; then they and their ideas are ambushed by a reality that makes their discussion look idle. You have some classical notions of how evil works; then you need a prayer. "Angels and ministers of grace defend us!" Event overtakes theory.

As well as surprise, there is dislocation. Scenes can be arranged in a way that doesn't merely perplex the characters, but also disturbs the audience. In the second scene of the play, it has been suggested that the audience may not be sure quite where to look. The second scene of the play is totally different from the first. It's day, not night; we're in a formal court scene, not a few soldiers doing sentry duty. We have long ceremonial speeches from the King, not short speeches and interrupted ideas. But we in the audience, in that second scene, are required to choose from, or keep switching between, two points of view. Are we to look at Claudius? He's the king, he's on the throne, he's got the crown and the robes. He's got nearly all the lines, and everybody else is listening to him and doing exactly what he says. Or are we to look at Hamlet? Over on the side, there's a young man dressed in black, saying nothing for a very long time, but he's the most famous young actor in England, and it's his performance that we came to see.

We are presented with puzzles. The play is full of puzzles; the play is, in fact, full of questions. One of Hamlet's most distinguished critics, Maynard Mack, great professor at Yale, wrote an essay called "The World of Hamlet," which I reread every time I teach the play. He observed that much of the play is written in the interrogative mood. It is full of literal questions. The opening line of the play is "Who's there?" Very soon after that, Horatio says the line I've already quoted: "What, has this thing appeared again tonight?" Or a deeper question, Hamlet's inquiry, "Yet what to me is this quintessence of dust?" or "What should such fellows as I do crawling between earth and heaven?" or "Now Hamlet, where's Polonius?" which is not a simple question, because Polonius is at the moment dead, and you wonder where Polonius is. Or the biggest one of all, "To be or not to be? That is the question."

Maybe that's not the biggest one of all. That leads to the biggest one of all: what happens after we die? C.S. Lewis, in another brilliant essay on *Hamlet*, which I also reread regularly—it's called "Hamlet: The Prince or the Poem"—has written that death could be considered the subject of this play. By that, he does not mean that most of the characters die. That's true in most tragedies. But in most tragedies, death is the end, the frame, the limit. Death may be defeat, it may be deliverance, it may even be victory, but it is the last thing in the play. In *Hamlet*, however, our attention is frequently drawn to the state of being dead. What happens after death, in that "country from whose bourne no traveler returns?" Hamlet worries about the fate of Claudius's soul. If he kills the King while the King is praying, will he go straight to Heaven? What revenge is that?

The ghost gives a glimpse of the fires of Purgatory. The dying Hamlet himself is anxious that Horatio should survive to tell his story, else, "what a wounded name" I will leave behind. We worry not only about the fate of the soul and the fate of the name, the reputation, but also the fate of the body. Is Ophelia's corpse entitled to full rites of burial? Will Polonius's corpse be feasted on by a convocation of politic worms? How long will a corpse last in the ground? A tanner's corpse will last nine years, longer than anyone else. Is the noble dust of Alexander now stopping the bunghole of a beer barrel? The questions are pressing. They are also unanswerable, for unless you short-circuit the process by an act of faith, by professing a religious belief, we cannot know what it is to be dead. None of us has ever been dead, although all of us eventually will be.

The questioning reaches its highest pitch, its furthest range, because of the ghost. He could tell us what being dead is like. Apparently one traveler has returned from that bourne, that undiscovered country. Any critical comment on the play of *Hamlet* that shortcuts the ghost, that ignores the ghost, de-emphasizes it, that pretends that Hamlet could have found out about his father's murder by some ordinary means, discovering some evidence, some physical clues, does not pay attention to a play whose whole first act is organized around the ghost.

The ghost of Hamlet's father is the most successful ghost in Elizabethan drama. It is a dreaded sight, an apparition. It reveals an unexpected dimension to the universe, and it remains permanently a thing of fear and wonder. It keeps doing unexpected things. Naturally enough, scholars of Shakespeare have inquired what do the Elizabethans think of ghosts, what veracity could Hamlet reasonably attribute to this messenger from another world. When scholars have inquired into this, they have found a very pretty puzzle indeed. They have found a conflict of opinion.

In general, Catholics said that ghosts came from Purgatory. Purgatory is that middle place in the afterworld, between Heaven and Hell, where a soul that is repentant, but isn't doomed to everlasting damnation, but hasn't been extremely good either, will purge itself of its earthly crimes and make itself fit for Heaven. Some such spirits might be permitted to revisit the earth, requesting of a living man some earthly action that would assist them in finding rest. Since they could come back to the earth only with divine permission, living men might rightly obey their command.

Protestants thought differently. They thought the ghosts did appear, but they didn't come from Purgatory. In fact, one of the things that Protestantism did was to abolish the whole doctrine of Purgatory; there was no such place. When you died, you went straight to Hell or to Heaven, no other possibilities. Therefore, a ghost either came from Heaven, but that was very rare indeed. Most ghosts came from Hell, and they were really not the ghosts of your relatives. A ghost was really a demon, who assumed the appearance of your dead relative, and its purpose was to ensnare your soul into damnation.

There was a third view, and this could be espoused either by a Catholic or by a Protestant, or by just general skeptics who sat more lightly to religious matters. Some ghosts are mere hallucinations. Melancholy people like Hamlet, people who have been through disturbing circumstances, and are in unusual states of mind, are particularly prone to seeing ghosts. They conjure the ghosts out of their own mental distress. A ghost was an index of an unsound mind.

The fascinating thing about the ghost in *Hamlet* is that Shakespeare doesn't make up his mind about those possibilities. He doesn't need to, after all; doctrine about ghosts is not amongst the most important things, where you have to get it right or you'll be damned. It isn't central to theology. Most people's minds were probably jumbled on it. Shakespeare's mind seems to have been jumbled, but in his case it was an artistic jumble. The ghost describes its own condition in largely Catholic terms. It says it dwells in a prisonhouse, where its foul crimes of life are burnt and purged away. That sounds like Purgatory, but not all of the details are consistent. It starts like a guilty thing, upon the crowing of a cock, and it requests blood revenge. These do not sound like the actions of a repentant spirit. Hamlet later contemplates the possibility that the ghost is a devil, the Protestant view. He says "The devil hath power / To assume a pleasing shape;" it may be abusing me to damn me, telling me lies in order to draw me into Hell. That's why he feels he must test Claudius' guilt by some other means, the "mousetrap" play. The hallucination theory comes up several times. It is Horatio's first opinion—"'Tis your fantasy"—and when the ghost last appears in Gertrude's bedchamber, Hamlet can see it and hear it; Gertrude can see nothing and thinks it's Hamlet's fantasy.

Shakespeare uses the variety of Renaissance views on the ghost to give Hamlet a problem. He exploits the conflict of opinion to create real uncertainty, agonizing and important doubt, doubt that we share. After all, it's his business as a playwright not to tell us what to believe about ghosts, but to give us the experience of encountering a ghost, to put us in exactly the same position as Hamlet—what ontological status does this apparition have?—which forces us into an intense identification with the Prince. The ghost certainly does exist. It does exist; Hamlet is not the only one to see it. The other soldiers and Horatio see it. But he is the only one to hear what it says.

The truth of its message is questionable. If it is what it says it is, and comes with divine authority, then it does two things, both of which are overwhelming. First, it reveals to Hamlet abysses of evil in the world beyond those that he already suspected; he was already upset about his father's death and his mother's quick remarriage to a man he detests, his uncle. Now he's finding out that his father has been murdered. It also imposes upon Hamlet an absolute command to a decisive and devastating action, namely to kill his uncle, the present King of Denmark. On the other hand, if the ghost were not what it says it is, if its message is false, Hamlet would do great evil to obey it. His imagination would be "as foul / As Vulcan's stithy," and he has all the more obligation to resist its commands because he would like to obey it anyway; he hates and loathes Claudius.

The ghost is in some sense real; it is also ambiguous. It is also very dangerous, because it reinforces Hamlet's already developed feelings and drives him toward an action that would be utterly villainous if it were not endorsed by a supernatural command. Hamlet's famous delay, whatever else may contribute to it, originates in the ambiguity and peril of the ghost. He's utterly convinced by it when he's in direct encounter with it, naturally enough; whatever the ghost may be, it's overwhelming, and it sure looks like Daddy. But when the ghost leaves, Hamlet must consider the alternatives before he proceeds to action.

Lecture Twenty-Six
Hamlet: The Causes of Tragedy

Scope:

The characters in *Hamlet* are remarkably thoughtful. Indeed, Hamlet himself is the only Shakespearean hero whose university we know. The lecture explores the Renaissance linkage of education, the classics, and the theater. It then proceeds to analyze Hamlet's own exploration of the causes of tragedy: Aristotle's theory of tragic flaw, Boethius' theory of fortune, and Isaiah's theory of divine ministers.

Outline

I. *Hamlet* is an intellectual and epistemological play distinguished by its thoughtful and reflective speeches.

    A. Older characters—Polonius and Claudius—give long speeches of advice.

    B. Younger characters—Hamlet, Horatio, Rosencrantz, Guildenstern—are university students.

II. *Hamlet* manifests interests in education, in the classics, and in the theater, sometimes linking the three: Hamlet evidently saw the Players enact a play on a classical subject at Wittenberg.

    A. Wittenberg was one of the new universities of the Renaissance, founded by Frederick the Wise, Elector of Saxony, in 1502. It was particularly concerned with humanism and with Protestantism.

        1. Martin Luther took a degree at this university.

        2. It is also the university of the fictional character Doctor Faustus.

    B. Shakespeare's play seems particularly to have interested a university audience in its own time: it was performed at Oxford and Cambridge and earned the praise of a Cambridge don, Gabriel Harvey.

III. The range of Hamlet's mind and education is clear in his efforts to explain the causes of evil.

    A. In Act 1 Scene 4, he explores Aristotle's theory of the tragic flaw (*hamartia*). We need to ask whether Shakespeare construct his own tragedies on the basis of this theory.

B. In Act 2 Scene 2, Hamlet's request for a speech on the fall of Troy leads to a speech on Boethius' theory (propounded in the early sixth century A.D.) that Fortune is the cause of tragic falls.

    1. Invoking Troy leads us back to the archetypal tragic story.

    2. Kenneth Branagh's casting of John Gielgud and Judi Dench as Priam and Hecuba in his movie of *Hamlet* supports that sense of going back to older tragic models.

C. In Act 3 Scene 4, Hamlet invokes the prophetic theory, to be found in Isaiah, that God selects human agents to serve as scourges and ministers dealing with evil on earth.

    1. King Richard III is an example of the former.

    2. Richmond, future King Henry, is an example of the latter.

    3. Hamlet combines prophet and minister in one person.

IV. Hamlet's wide-ranging search for the origins of tragedy has been followed by many critics seeking the reasons for Hamlet's own troubles.

A. Goethe suggested that Hamlet was too delicate, too sensitive.

B. Coleridge thought that Hamlet was constitutionally given to thought and indisposed to action.

C. The critic Kitto suggested that Hamlet was too shocked by his father's death and mother's rapid remarriage to his uncle to do anything.

D. Freud held that Hamlet was unable to revenge himself on his uncle because Claudius has carried out his own (Hamlet's) Oedipal fantasy.

Essential Reading:

Shakespeare, *Hamlet*.

Supplementary Reading:

Edwards, Introduction to *Hamlet* (New Cambridge edition).

Goldman, *Shakespeare and the Energies of Drama*, chapter 6.

Questions to Consider:

1. Consider the analyses of Hamlet in Paragraph IV of the outline. Which one(s) do you agree with? Explain your reasons. Can you come up with any reason for Hamlet's troubles not mentioned in the lecture?

2. Why is Hamlet's status as a university (drop-out) student significant?

Lecture Twenty-Six—Transcript
Hamlet: The Causes of Tragedy

I ended the last lecture by saying that *Hamlet* is full of questions. It is an intellectual play, an epistemological play. We ask what can we know, how we can we be sure that we know what we know. It is a play where people talk about their ideas at great length. The older characters are given to thoughtful and reflective speeches. In the second scene of the play, Claudius has a very long speech on how to handle grief; he tells Hamlet that it is very proper to grieve for his dead father, but to grieve too long is unmanly. "It shows a will most incorrect to heaven" and so forth and so on; very long, paternal and avuncular advice. Polonius gets his chance with Laertes later on in the first act, with a very famous speech about how he should behave himself when he's traveling abroad in Paris, ending with "This above all: to thine own self be true."

The younger characters are themselves intellectuals. Rosencrantz and Guildenstern were school-fellows of Hamlet. In the First Quarto of the play, it's made quite clear that this means they have been at the University of Wittenburg with him. In the Second Quarto, it's school-fellows "of their young days brought up with him"—it sounds more like a childhood friendship than a college friendship. Horatio has certainly been at college with Hamlet; the two of them have been philosophy students at the University of Wittenburg. Of all Shakespeare's plays, this one most ostentatiously flaunts an interest in higher education, an interest in the university. Moreover, it links the university to the classics, which were, of course, taught at the universities, and links both the universities and the classics to the theater. Several times in the play, we hear about classical stories that get reenacted on the stage at the university. Polonius, when he was a university student, played the role of Julius Caesar; he was killed in the capitol. Hamlet has evidently seen the traveling players who turn up in Elsinore at Wittenburg. They are not native to Denmark, and Wittenburg is apparently the only other place he has been. Moreover, he remembers them performing a play about the fall of Troy, and asks the chief player to deliver a speech from that play when they arrive at Elsinore.

I should say more about Wittenburg before I go further, because I think there are reasons why Shakespeare is so specific in naming it. Many of Shakespeare's leading characters are witty and educated people, but Hamlet is the only case with a leading character where we are specifically told what university he went to. Wittenburg was one of the new universities of the Renaissance, founded in the year 1502 by Frederick the Wise, Elector of Saxony. That is, it was not quite a century old at the time that Shakespeare write the play. Wittenburg was especially associated with the new humanism. Frederick and the men he appointed to run Wittenburg were eager to stock the university library with classical texts, to buy up all the first editions, the first printed editions of classical texts that came out from the Aldine Press in Venice.

It was also associated, from very early on, with Protestantism. Martin Luther earned a theological degree at Wittenburg. That's historical fact. In historical fiction, Wittenburg was the university of the man who mastered all branches of knowledge, Doctor Faustus. It's an appropriate university for Hamlet to have gone to, an appropriate university for a man who struggles in a way unlike any other Shakespearean hero with moral, philosophical and religious dilemmas. Shakespeare's own play had a university connection; that First Quarto edition of the play that came out in 1603. It's a defective text; it's only about two-thirds of the length of the Second Quarto that came out a couple of years later. But it has something very interesting on the title page. It says, "As was enacted at the two universities of Oxford and Cambridge." This is the only case where we know for sure that Shakespeare's play was acted at the English universities in his own time. The play earned the praise of a university don, a man named Gabriel Harvey, at Cambridge. Harvey was a vain and waspish man, always getting into quarrels, couldn't get promotion even at Cambridge, let alone find a job anywhere else. He was the kind of perfect academic nasty man and was very reluctant to praise anything. But, he wrote privately in his own notes a praise of this play. He said that, Shakespeare's, … "the younger sort take much delight in Shakespeare's *Venus and Adonis*"—a long, sexy, romantic poem—"but his tragedy of *Hamlet, Prince of Denmark* hath it in him to please the wiser sort." That's a wonderful comment. I'm very fond of that. It's self-gratifying; I like *Hamlet*, therefore I must be of the wiser sort.

The play has its university links, and Hamlet is very much a university man. This is one of the reasons why Hamlet is a favorite character amongst my students; they identify with him. They are going through some of the Hamlet experiences. They themselves are university students. Hamlet's the most famous dropout, of course, in English literature; his parents don't let him go back to the University. He's got a mind that's been trained by the University. The range of his mind and the effect of his education are clear in his own effort to understand and explain why evil things are happening in Denmark. He puts his learning to use in trying to analyze his own situation.

As I said in an earlier lecture, one of those moving and compelling things in Shakespeare lies in the character's own efforts to grasp the nature of tragedy. Let me go back to a speech I quoted in the previous lecture, the speech in which he talks about Claudius' drinking, and generalizes about the effect of "a vicious mole of nature," one fault in a nation or a person. "A vicious mole":

> The stamp of one defect,
>
> Being nature's livery, or fortune's star—
>
> Their virtues else—be they as pure as grace,
>
> As infinite as man may undergo—
>
> Shall in the general censure take corruption
>
> From that particular fault.

His discussion of Claudius' drinking habit leads him into something that sounds like an academic exposition of Aristotle's notion of tragic flaw. He knows he's digressing, getting way off the subject. It had begun simply with Horatio asking why are those guns going off, and he answered, "Because the King like firing cannon off when he toasts, when he drinks." He is getting way off the subject, because Hamlet would never admit that Claudius has only one fault, and is otherwise possessed of a host of virtues. He's more interested in the theory than in the occasion. He's passing a time of waiting by discussing some ideas that he acquired at the University. He's probably recalling a lecture he heard at Wittenburg, where Herr Doktor Professor Heinrich von Weltschmerz was reading out of the Aldine edition of 1508, published six years before the university was founded, with the Latin commentaries of Robortello, Castelvetro and Pazzi about Aristotle's theory of, in, the *Poetics*.

In fact, Hamlet himself becomes nearly as fussy and pedantic as the dryest-dust professor can get. In his final sentence in his speech about the vicious mole, he enters into the unintelligibility of a professor who's totally lost in his own topic. His final sentence is, "the dram of eale / Doth all the noble substance of a doubt / To his own scandal." What? What is a "dram of eale?" What's "of a doubt?" Where's the verb in that sentence? Scholars have wondered and written desperate annotations and emendations of that line. Never mind.

Some students have seen the presence in the play of this whole speech as a warrant for saying that *hamartia*, tragic flaw, is a key notion in Shakespearean tragedy, that we can fully understand Hamlet and other Shakespearean tragic heroes by identifying their tragic errors. In fact, Laurence Olivier, in his movie version of *Hamlet* in the 1940s, had recited this speech over the credits at the beginning of the film. We are all familiar with this theory of tragic flaw. We learn it at school when we first read tragedy. It is a useful theory; people do have flaws, and they often suffer as a result of them. But I want to handle this theory of tragic flaw with great care. In my experience of Shakespeare, and particularly of students reading Shakespeare and writing papers about him, the usefulness of the theory of tragic flaw is limited. Some of my students have thought that the tragic hero is supposed to have only one fault. It usually turns out to be pride, and the whole of tragic drama is reduced to one long, boring sermon against pride. Or the student assumes that the flaw is the most important thing about the character, and we need not bother to observe his virtues, or even admit that he has any. Or, the flaw must be responsible for all the suffering in a tragedy, that none of it will come about through the evil deeds of other characters or through chance.

This sort of reasoning ends up denying the abundance of Shakespeare, denying the richness of his characterization. It also ends up in absurd positions. For example, I've read papers that make me think you could be a monstrous villain, a tyrannical conqueror—sacking cities, raping maidens, performing all sorts of horrible cruelties on people—and die peacefully in your bed. But, if you're one of those decent chaps who just happens to have a tragic flaw, then the gods in total justice will pound you into atoms. If that's what tragedy has to teach us, I'll go back to reading Mother Goose; she's wiser about human affairs than that. Or it ends up in what may be worse, a kind of self-righteousness, a kind of putting-down of the tragic hero in favor of ourselves. A critic writes a paper, and Julius Caesar has conquered the world. He's therefore become very egotistical and pompous; therefore, he deserves to be assassinated. The implication is that I, the critic, if I were lucky enough to conquer the world, would be very mild and benevolent about my success, and nobody would have any reason to fear or hate me.

The notion of tragic flaw is useful for explaining occasional scenes in Shakespeare. Certainly, the characters do have flaws, and the flaws have consequences. But it's too small a theory to account for the richness of a Shakespearean play. Certainly, one flaw in Hamlet cannot explain the whole rottenness of Denmark. Shakespeare knew the theory of tragic flaw, obviously. He shows he knows it right in this passage. But for him, as for other Elizabethan writers, it doesn't seem to have been a ruling concept. When they theorized about tragedy, which, as I've mentioned, they didn't often do, they often resorted not to a classical idea, but to a medieval idea, an idea most influentially expressed by the early medieval philosopher Boethius.

Boethius was early medieval, or perhaps the last of the classical writers. He's early sixth century; he lived in Rome. He was a Roman nobleman, who had a terrible fall. His family was distinguished, his father had been a consul, he himself was a senator and a consul, and lived to see both of his sons consuls, all this under the Gothic emperors who'd taken over Italy in the sixth century. Then, Boethius was accused of something (we know not what), thrown into prison, kept there a while, tortured and put to death. While he was in prison, he wrote a book called *The Consolation of Philosophy*, out of his own experience; how philosophy can console us in time of misfortune. That book became one of the most influential books to come down from late classical times. Everybody knew it; everybody read it who read anything at all. It got translated into English by three very distinguished people: King Alfred the Great, Geoffrey Chaucer, and Queen Elizabeth.

It is Boethius that is responsible for a widespread notion that misfortune derives from an irrational power called *fortuna*, the goddess Fortuna. She is in charge of human life, and she gives us tragic events. To quote Boethius, in English translation, "What else does the cry of tragedy bewail but the overthrow of happy realms by the unexpected blow of Fortune?" Fortune is a personification of the idiotic mutability of the world. She is a strumpet goddess. She gives her gifts, and then she takes them away, unpredictably, irrationally. She, by the way, has already been mentioned earlier in the play of *Hamlet*, in Hamlet's first encounter with Rosencrantz and Guildenstern, when Rosencrantz and Guildenstern claim to live in the middle parts of Fortune, not high on Fortune's wheel, nor low, but in the middle parts. "Faith, her privates we," they say as a kind of dirty joke. When Hamlet asks the Player to recite a speech on the fall of Troy, that speech turns out to end with an outcry against the power of Fortune.

> Out, out, thou strumpet Fortune! All you gods,
>
> In general synod take away her power;
>
> Break all the spokes and fellies from her wheel,
>
> And bowl the round nave down the hill of heaven,
>
> As low as to the fiends!

One of the reasons why Hamlet asks for that particular speech may be that he wants to hear the theory of Fortune fully expressed. This could be an explanation for the rottenness of Denmark.

Another reason why he may want that particular speech also related to his education, because it is a speech about the fall of Troy. This story is the original tragic story in the West. All of Greek tragedy comes out of the fall of Troy. The *Iliad* is the first surviving work of European literature, and the Greek tragic playwrights derived their plots from Homer and from the associated myths. If we go back to Priam and Hecuba, the death of Priam and the mourning of Hecuba, maybe we can understand something about what's happening in Denmark, particularly because that story centers on Pyrrhus Neoptolemus, the son of Achilles, who assaulted Troy and killed Priam as a revenge for the death of his father, Achilles, who had been killed before the gates of Troy. That sense of Hamlet going back to the roots of tragic experience is very strong in this passage, and it is a matter that Kenneth Branagh underscored particularly, when he made his film version of Hamlet a couple of years ago.

If you have seen that film, you will remember that he shows Priam and Hecuba. Over the speeches, we have some images of the fall of Troy. King Priam is played by John Gielgud, and Hecuba is played by Judi Dench. That's a very interesting effect indeed, because John Gielgud, who was the great Hamlet of the first half of the twentieth century, is now in his 90s. Judi Dench, who played all the young Shakespearean female leads a generation ago, is now in her 60s. Branagh, making this film, was in his 30s. He's gotten the two previous generations of great tragic actors to back him up in that movie. "Can you help me, Sir John? Can you help me, Dame Judi?

Can you give the real tragic thing for me as I try to do this play too? Can you help me understand this play that I'm putting on?" That's the kind of context that Hamlet is evoking in his own play, and Branagh found an unusual and marvelous way to express it.

Let me return to fortune, however, Boethius' idea; Fortune causes tragedy. Fortune is certainly a thorough explanation for earthly events. Perhaps it is too thorough an explanation. If everything is sheer happenstance, then nothing is explicable. There's no sense to be found, and any human action would be as irrational as Fortune itself. That is, if we concede that everything is Fortune, you've got no explanations left at all; it's too big, as the tragic flaw is too small.

Let us go on to another possibility. A third view of tragedy arises later in the play, in the closet scene, the scene where Hamlet confronts his mother in her bedroom and accidentally kills Polonius; he doesn't even know Polonius is there. When he picks up the body of Polonius to take him out near the end of the scene, he says:

> For this same lord,
>
> I do repent; but heaven hath pleas'd it so,
>
> To punish me with this, and this with me,
>
> That I must be their scourge and minister.

It pleases heaven to punish me with this—people like Polonius getting in my way—and this with me; Polonius gets punished by this, so I am a scourge and minister in Denmark. This is a new, a different view of tragedy, a view that tragedy is part of God's plan, God's way of coping with evil in the world. God intervenes in human affairs to see that justice is done. In some cases, He intervenes by means of a human agent. That is, He picks a particular man to punish others for their crimes, using one human being to bring another, justifiably, from prosperity to misery. Such a divine agent could be described with one of two nouns, either a scourge or a minister, depending on his own ethical status.

A scourge is usually a man who is already so wicked himself that he is beyond salvation. The wickedness he does in punishing other miscreants adds no more to his crimes; God can use him as an agent. It doesn't corrupt him anymore; indeed, his function in the divine plan is part of his own punishment. "He punishes me with this." That is what Richard III is in the play of *Richard III*; he is God's agent upon the Yorkists and the Lancastrians, to punish them for all their sins in the Wars of the Roses. He's the worst of them all, and he can go to Hell having done all that. A minister is also an agent of God, but his ethical status is different. A minister punishes—"to punish this with me"—but he does not merely punish. He also sets up a new situation that is good. Where a scourge merely wreaks the wrath of God, a minister purges the whole guilty condition, and circumstances are so arranged that his infliction of punishment on others is not in itself a further crime, but an act of public justice. If Richard III is the scourge in that play, then Henry Richmond, who is going to become Henry Tudor, King of England, is the minister, the new guy, the good guy, the guy in shining armor.

Richard III is a fairly simple play compared to *Hamlet*. Shakespeare has neatly separated the role of scourge from the role of minister. Hamlet is more complicated, and Hamlet himself, the prince, sees that it is hard to be a scourge without being a minister, and hard to be a minister without being a scourge. Things are messy here. It is difficult to get into this business of divine vengeance without getting guilty yourself. This execution of divine command is physically messy and morally risky. By the way, I haven't attached a name to this idea yet, as I attached the name of Aristotle to tragic flaw and Boethius to Fortune. The name that should be attached to this is Isaiah. This is a prophetic theory, first fully expressed in the book of the prophet Isaiah in the Hebrew Bible, where he describes King Cyrus, Cyrus the Mede, as God's agent to overthrow the tyranny of Nebuchadnezzar and allow the Jews to go back to their promised land.

I hope I'm not confusing you. What I'm trying to do is point out to you how Hamlet introduces to the play, introduces to the events of the play, a variety of explanations for tragic occurrences: the Aristotelian theory of corrupting flaw; the medieval theory, in Boethius, of destructive Fortune; the Isaiahan theory of providential intervention of human affairs. Hamlet embodies a whole range of intellectual responses to his situation. For Hamlet, the ancient past is usable. He's an educated humanist, free to range among the ancient pieces of wisdom that Wittenburg has made available to him. He will use a passage of literary criticism like Aristotle, a passage of philosophy like Boethius, or a passage of history and instruction. Isaiah would be considered in the Renaissance as both history—because it's talking about real historical events, the Babylonian captivity, King Cyrus the Great and so forth—and instruction, because it is prophecy and tells Israel and eventually Christians how to behave.

He will use criticism, philosophy, history and teaching for the potential explanation of his own circumstances. Ancient writings speak directly to him. I find that intensely interesting. I'm a professor; for me, literary criticism serves to make judgments, to increase knowledge, to understand texts, to help others to read more sensitively with more understanding. But for Hamlet, literary criticism serves to help him understand what is going on around him, to help him understand his life. Literary criticism helps him know what kind of story he is in. It is a marvelous use for literary criticism. Hamlet's wide-ranging search for the origins of tragedy has been, of course, followed by many critics reading the play of *Hamlet* itself, seeking the reasons for Hamlet's own troubles.

What is the matter with Hamlet himself? We have been asking, we have eagerly been discussing for about three centuries. People started saying, in the eighteenth century, it seems that no sufficient reason is given Hamlet for his delay in killing Claudius. The great minds that have read Shakespeare since then have offered reasons, rather paralleling the activity of Hamlet himself. Goethe, at the beginning of the nineteenth century, suggested that Hamlet was too delicate, too gentle a man. He compared Hamlet to a fine porcelain vase in which an acorn has been planted. As the acorn grows into an oak, of course, the porcelain vase will be shattered. The circumstances of Denmark are too tough for a man of Hamlet's fine constitution. Coleridge, in England some years later, gave a different twist to that. He thought that Hamlet was a man constitutionally given to thought, to meditation, to argument, indisposed to action. That's why he can't do what the ghost tells him; he's not an active sort of man. Coleridge went on to say, "I think I have a smack of Hamlet in me too." Actually, most people who talk about Hamlet project themselves into Hamlet in one way or another. I was just doing that, as you may have noticed, in talking about how Hamlet uses literary criticism. There was something of me in that.

In the twentieth century, a great Oxford scholar named Kitto observed that Hamlet is too shocked by the death of his father, and deeply horrified by his mother's rapid and tasteless marriage; that's what stops him from doing anything. Freud observed, of course, that

Hamlet was unable to avenge himself on his uncle because his uncle had done exactly what he unconsciously wanted to do—namely, kill the father and marry the mother. You cannot kill out of moral outrage a man who has fulfilled your own subconscious desires. Other critics have suggested that Hamlet is inhibited by genuine ethical concerns; it is wrong to kill people. Revenge is wrong, and Hamlet is puzzled by the ethics of revenge. I am listing these explanations at the moment. You can find, in the text of *Hamlet*, support for each one of those. The Freudian theory looks very good indeed in the closet scene with Gertrude. The trouble with each of them is that it's hard to find consistent support throughout the play. These are suggestions made about Hamlet in various different places of the play, as Hamlet himself comes up with various suggestions about tragedy in various different places in the play. The play doesn't seem to support any of them all the way through.

Lecture Twenty-Seven
Hamlet: The Protestant Hero

Scope:

This lecture first discusses the king and the queen and the variety of interpretation that they may provoke. It then turns to Hamlet himself and describes him as an embodiment of the variety and problems of young manhood. Hamlet is especially linked with certain ideals of the Renaissance and certain problems arising from the Protestant rejection of earthly authorities.

Outline

I. Claudius has been played in a variety of ways, from the repulsive king of Basil Sydney in Laurence Olivier's film to the able and affable king of Patrick Stewart in the BBC-TV videotape.

    A. However he is played, his guilt, although not necessarily obvious at first, becomes clear, and may be tragic and moving in the prayer scene.

    B. Claudius shows us the picture of the usurper, guilty of the "oldest primal curse" of fratricide, and what he does to himself because of this.

II. The extent of Gertrude's awareness of what is going on in Elsinore is not clear in the script.

    A. Her knowledge may be clarified by performances such as that given by Glenn Close in the duel scene of Zeffirelli's film and Julie Christie in the closet scene of Branagh's film.

    B. The part of Gertrude is really underwritten.

III. Hamlet's tragedy is the tragedy of youth. He is trying to cope with problems not of his creation.

    A. He contrasts with the middle-aged Macbeth and the old Lear.

    B. He has trouble coordinating his excellent mind and education with his passionate feelings and impulses.

    C. He admires both the stoical Horatio and the emotional Player.

    D. His feelings about Ophelia veer from love to profound mistrust.

        1. In the grave scene, he professes his love.

    2. But earlier, when he is suspicious of her, he actually insults her.

    E. In one soliloquy he first rages at Claudius and then mocks his own rage.

IV. Hamlet embodies Protestant doubts and anxieties, the isolated soul without the clear guides provided by the Catholic Middle Ages.

    A. His soliloquy ("what a piece of work is man") shows an awareness of medieval humanistic doctrine, yet he can't assent to it.

    B. Upon his return from the sea voyage, however, he shows a belief in the divine governance of the world ("There is special providence in the fall of a sparrow").

        1. Hamlet stops trying to control things from this juncture forward.

        2. Since God governs all things, we do not need to look for explanation in theories (e.g., Aristotle, Boethius, Isaiah).

        3. Rather, "readiness is all," and Hamlet is now ready to act.

Essential Reading:

Shakespeare, *Hamlet*.

Supplementary Reading:

Kitto, *Form and Meaning in Drama*, chapter 9.

Lewis, "Hamlet—The Prince or the Poem."

Rose, "*Hamlet*—the 'Mona Lisa' of Literature."

Questions to Consider:

1. In line with this lecture's title, assess Hamlet as a "Protestant hero." Why is it important to make this distinction, especially since there is no overt theology or religion in the play? Can Hamlet be considered a hero in any other context?

2. The lecture also points up the fact that Hamlet is a young "hero" whose doubts and impetuosity war with each other. One observer said that the play could be summed up by two maxims: "Look before you leap" and "he who hesitates is lost." Identify key junctures in the play where Hamlet "looks" and where he "leaps." What are the consequences of these actions at these points? What might have happened if he reversed the actions?

Lecture Twenty-Seven—Transcript
Hamlet: The Protestant Hero

The variety that exists in the play of *Hamlet* lies not only in the situation in Denmark and in the title character, but in the other major characters as well. Before I go on and talk more about the Prince himself, I should say something about Claudius and about Gertrude. The role of the king is open to interpretation in a number of ways; it isn't a set thing. Perhaps I can make this most clear if I use two famous performances of the part that are available to anyone who has a VCR: the performance of Basil Sydney in Laurence Olivier's film of *Hamlet*; and the performance available on the BBC-TV version of it, which has Derek Jacobi as the prince and Patrick Stewart as the king.

Basil Sydney's performance was governed by the angle of the whole Olivier film; Olivier interpreted the film in a Freudian sense. Hamlet had an Oedipal complex; therefore, he detested Claudius. And Claudius was looked at largely from Hamlet's point of view; therefore, Claudius was exceedingly ugly. There were no particular politics in that film. All the arrangements with Norway, all the intrigue with Rosencrantz and Guildenstern, all that was cut out of the script. There was nothing, in fact, in particular for Claudius to do except be ugly from Hamlet's point of view. Thus, Basil Sydney, although he was an ordinarily attractive actor who had played Hamlet himself in his younger days, looked quite repulsive—harsh lines to the face, with very severe eyebrows and a full horizontal mustache, and a beard that jutted out instead of going down; his face looked like a squashed frog. He drank disgustingly and tossed away the goblet as if he were Henry VIII throwing chicken bones over his shoulder. In general, he was what Hamlet called the "mildewed ear," the "bloat king." He was meant to contrast with Gertrude, who in that case was a ravishing young woman, younger, indeed, than Olivier himself, whom Hamlet could clearly lust after. That extreme, the Basil Sydney bloat king, the mildewed ear, the ugly man that squats upon the throne, contrasts enormously with the Claudius created by Patrick Stewart.

Patrick Stewart, before he became a star of *Star Trek*, had a very distinguished Shakespearean career with the Royal Shakespeare Company, played all sorts of leads, had played Claudius onstage before he did it for the BBC, and played Claudius as a most affable and charming man. In the first scene in which he appears, the first court scene, he is clearly in charge. He sends the ambassadors to Norway. He makes clear the limits of their power to them. He calls forth Laertes, he puts the Queen beside him, treats her very nicely. He does all these things, clearly in control, but not tyrannically. He does it with a genial authority. He is perceptive, affectionate, attentive, patient, as well as diplomatic, resourceful, and strong. In fact, I've taken that list of adjectives from Stewart's own description of the part; he wrote an essay about playing Claudius. Therefore, we see an able king, a king who is able to cope with Denmark's position in the international world, diffuse the threat of Fortinbras in Norway, a king who is alert about Hamlet and his problems, and genuinely concerned to cope with them, a king who is genuinely in love with Gertrude. Once it is clear that Hamlet hates him and is going to cause all sorts of trouble, this enormously resourceful king could have killed Hamlet; after all, he killed Hamlet's father without there being suspicion, he could kill Hamlet as well. But Gertrude loves young Hamlet, and he doesn't want to upset her.

It became a most interesting portrait of what a usurper has done to himself, a fundamentally nice guy and capable man who got himself into trouble by usurping a crown and taking over a woman that wasn't his, and struggling ever after with the guilt. The prayer scene, as Patrick Stewart played it, was most moving: "O, my offence is rank, it smells to heaven; / It hath the eldest primal curse upon't, / A brother's murder!" Claudius knows very well what he's done; he's done the wickedest thing possible. The "eldest primal curse" is the curse of Cain—Cain, who committed the first murder, murdered his good brother. He is guilty, and he knows he's guilty, and he knows he will go to Hell if he does not repent.

He cannot quite bring himself to repent, because that would mean giving up the profits of his crime: his crown, his ambition, and above all, his queen, and he cannot bring himself to do that. He's a man who slowly grows harder, doesn't want to do nasty things, but must do them. It can be a most moving performance; if we have any time at all to spare from Hamlet's dilemmas, we can be moved by Claudius. Shakespeare had written about this situation a number of times before, the usurping king and what happens to him. The most brilliant earlier example is Bolingbroke, who turns into King Henry IV and must cope with the results of his own usurpation. One of the results is what the usurper does to himself. Shakespeare's breadth of vision is enough to take in Claudius as well as Hamlet. Of course, the play does chiefly focus upon Hamlet. I'm not rewriting it as the tragedy of Claudius, but I must move on to Gertrude before I turn to Hamlet.

Gertrude is more difficult. It is a distinctly underwritten part. We wonder how much Gertrude knows of what her new husband has done, how much has gone on behind the scenes. It is an ambiguity in the play whether Gertrude slept with Claudius before her first husband died. The ghost says that Claudius "won the seeming virtue of my Queen," but it isn't absolutely explicit whether this was an adultery before the murder, or just a seduction prior to the marriage after the murder. How much does she know? She clearly does not know that her second husband killed her first. She seems to be utterly astonished when Hamlet, in the closet scene, says, "As bad a deed, good mother, / As kill a king and marry with his brother." Her response is, "As kill a king?"—"Who's been killing kings around here?"

The best suggestion I've had about the part of Gertrude came from an actor friend of mine, quite a distinguished actor, Austin Pendleton, who said to me, "I think it's a movie part, not a stage part." It's the kind of part in which a movie actress, without lines, can make all sorts of points because of the close-up camera, because Shakespeare didn't give her enough lines. I think that is borne out into other performances that I will mention. One is the performance of Glenn Close in the Zeffirelli version of *Hamlet*, the one that stars Mel Gibson. It is not Glenn Close's best performance; she's done many better movies. But the final scene, she's very good at. When she drinks the poisoned cup and realizes it's poisoned, she has a series of silent recognitions. She looks at Hamlet and realizes the poison must have been intended for him. She looks at Claudius and realizes that's where the poison must have come from. You can read on her face how she replays this whole story from the very beginning, from the death of her first husband, in the last 30 seconds of her life. Gertrude's realization, done without words, as a close-up camera effect, is a marvelous thing.

Even better, I think, is the performance of Julie Christie as Gertrude in the film made of *Hamlet* made by Kenneth Branagh. The bedroom scene—Julie Christie's Gertrude had been enjoying her second marriage. She has many new clothes; she has a gown and a new hairdo every scene she appears in. She is genuinely fond of her second husband, of Claudius, played in this case by Derek Jacobi, grown older. She is affectionate toward her son, but she's clearly taken up with the whirl and excitement of having a new husband, still being queen of Denmark, enjoying things being so prosperous, until we get to the closet scene. Her son starts raging against her, killing Polonius and leaving the body there in a huge pool of blood. She retreats onto the bed, and Julie Christie does this most marvelous thing of trying to sort out what's happening here, and realizing that she is partly at fault. She has not been thinking of the last couple of weeks from Hamlet's point of view. She has been worried about Hamlet being mad, but it hadn't occurred to her before that she might be partly at fault, her own behavior. She has failed in some way as a mother. She goes through one of those things that most mothers go through—most good mothers go through—when their children start misbehaving. "Did I do something wrong? Did I provoke this? Was the way I brought up this kid misdirected in some way?" These are moving moments that actresses can do. The script provides the room for it. It doesn't provide the firm direction for it. It must be the actress and the director who create this with Gertrude.

Let me go back to Hamlet himself. Hamlet is a young intellectual, I have been saying. He has been trying to cope with a set of appalling circumstances, circumstances for most of which he is not responsible. After all, the initial trouble in the play is the murder of his father, and he didn't cause that. His ideas have proved inadequate to guide him. Let me lay particular stress on his youth. If *King Lear* is the story, the tragedy of old age, the tragedy of a man who must let go and doesn't know how to let go, and *Macbeth* is the tragedy of a man in middle life, the man of some achievement in the world—he's settled, he's married, he's at the point where a man begins to wonder, "Is this it? Is this all I am going to achieve? Should I be satisfied with where I am?" If *Lear's* about old age, if *Macbeth* is about the middle years, then Hamlet certainly is young.

He suffers from a difficulty characteristic of intelligent young people, how to coordinate one's ideas with one's feelings. The people who complain that they don't understand Hamlet at all simply haven't been around college students enough. Hamlet is available to you in quantity on any university campus. Like most university students, Hamlet is stuffed with ideas: ideas from his education; ideas from his upbringing; ideas from his own reflection. However, the famous nineteenth-century image of Hamlet as a prince paralyzed by thought, Coleridge's prince, who just wants to think and not act, is only half true. He's also very passionate, very impulsive. His opening encounter with the ghost shows his ideas being violently displaced by his emotions, and his brushing Horatio aside, saying, "I'll make a ghost of anyone who stands in my way. I'm going to talk to that apparition."

For every thoughtful soliloquy he utters, he has a blaze of rash, fierce riot, stemming from the emotions that rage within him. He rages at his girlfriend, rages at his mother, stabs a sword through an arras to kill Polonius, without even bothering to find out who's behind that arras. Stealing a letter from Rosencrantz and Guildenstern and forging a replacement, which will send them to their deaths; fighting pirates; interrupting his own production of the mousetrap play with rude remarks; as we say now, Hamlet cannot get his act together. It is deeply significant that he has two enormous speeches of praise for other people, and they praise exactly opposite qualities. He praises the Player for his ability to express emotion with the utmost of freedom. The Player, in talking about Queen Hecuba, wept himself. Oh, that man can really let it all out, really let it go. Some 10 minutes later, he praises Horatio for being a Stoic; "all passions hit you, but you do not become passion's slave. I like a man like that; let me wear such a man in my heart of hearts." Both free expression and firm self-control earn his admiration.

That, I think, is why he's so mixed up about Ophelia. I don't have time to talk about Ophelia in detail, to talk about Ophelia from her own point of view, and that's unfair. From Hamlet's point of view, he's deeply conflicted between two opposite positions. One he expresses when she's dead, when he's quarreling with Laertes over the grave. "I loved Ophelia. Forty thousand brothers / Could not, with all their quantity of love, /Make up my sum like mine." There's never been any such love in the world of a young man for a young woman. Yet, earlier, in the nunnery scene, the moment he suspected that she might be the tool of her father and the king in getting it in, he abused her as a painted whore. "You jig, you amble, you lisp." This is clearly not what we call a mature relationship. She is either the most important person on earth, the most wonderful girl that ever was, or she's a traitor. I think you've seen young people go back and forth about their emotional commitment to a romantic object in that way; everything's either wonderful or, she let me down and she isn't worth a moment of my thought. which is to say that this doesn't have much to do with Ophelia. It's his own emotions that aren't very reliable. They're extremely forceful, but they're continually changing, and they're continually being undercut by his own intellect.

One of the stunning examples of that occurs in one of the soliloquies, when he's expressing his anger at Claudius. Having seen how emotional the Player could get, he bursts out in a similar rage about Claudius. "This is the way I should be talking about Claudius."

> It cannot be
>
> But I am pigeon-liver'd and lack gall
>
> To make oppression bitter, or ere this
>
> I should have fatted all the region kites
>
> With this slave's offal: bloody bawdy villain!
>
> Remorseless, lecherous, treacherous, kindless villain!
>
> O, vengeance!
>
> Why, what an ass am I! This is most brave,
>
> That I, the son of a dear father murder'd, ...
>
> Must unpack my heart with words, like a very whore.

It's that emotional break that I'm interested in; there's a great deal of Hamlet in that. The anger at Claudius was genuine; I don't think an actor can play that as fake; you've got to throw yourself into it, "Bloody bawdy villain! / Remorseless, treacherous, lecherous, kindless villain!" and the great cry at the end, "O, vengeance!" when Hamlet usually grabs a sword and waves it. At the same time, it is equally genuine for him to turn around and say, "What an ass am I!" –"I'm behaving like a character in a play," one of these old-fashioned revenge plays, where they hurl themselves around, chop off people's hands and are totally unconvincing. Hamlet rants, and the rant is genuine, but such is the quicksilver quality of human feeling that, after a couple of lines of rant, he perceives the rant to be rant and sneers at it.

Hamlet cannot maintain his own view, not until he takes the aborted trip to England. When he comes back from that adventure, then he is stabler. I think the way to sum this up is to go back to Wittenburg, to go to that Protestant university, Protestant humanist university that I started with. *Hamlet* the play and Hamlet the man are pervaded by a kind of intellectual doubt, characteristic of the Protestant Reformation. In the Catholic Middle Ages, the voice of God was heard clearly. God was knowable. Not totally known, of course—human beings can't totally know God—but sufficiently well known so that moral action can be straightforward. When the medieval mystery plays dramatized the sacrifice of Isaac, Abraham had no problem. Abraham is ordered to sacrifice his son. He's got an emotional problem, of course; he doesn't want to do it. He doesn't have an intellectual problem; he knows perfectly well that he must do it, that obedience to God is more important than paternal love. When the Protestant Reformation did away with all the intermediaries between God and man, when it did away with the hierarchy of the church offering an authoritative interpretation of the word of God, it left individuals alone with a limited ability to respond to a God who is not clearly known. Protestants believe in God's grace, but the principles by which grace operated were disputed in the Reformation. Insoluble moral questions arose: "What should I believe?", "When is God speaking to me?", "I can't take advice from a priest; it's got to come straight between me and God;" and "I'm not sure I'm hearing anything."

Hamlet has read books, he's taken notes, the University supplied plenty of learning, but he's still left uncertain how to apply it. We see him remember one piece of learning, "What a piece of work is a man," he says, "how noble in reason! how infinite in faculties! in form and moving how express and admirable! in action how like an angel! in apprehension how like a god! the beauty of the world, the paragon of animals! And yet to me what is this quintessence of dust?" The first part of that speech is orthodox Renaissance doctrine about man, about man's exalted position in the world, midway between the angels and the animals. It sounds very much, not like a German Protestant, but like an Italian philosopher, Picco della Mirandola, who wrote *An Oration on the Dignity of Man*, a thing that Hamlet would well have read at Wittenburg. Yet, vividly though he expresses the doctrine, Hamlet no longer assents to it. "What to me is this quintessence of dust?" To me, what is my particular position as a Protestant loner? There is the lonely Protestant voice full of lost idealism, nostalgia for the lost ideal.

Hamlet eventually does solve his problems. He solves them, apparently, on the boat to England. He discovers there that Rosencrantz and Guildenstern are carrying a letter sentencing him to death by the hand of the king of England. He manages to forge a substitute, and to make the substitute look genuine, because he just happens to be carrying in his pocket the Royal Seal, his father's signet that will authenticate the false orders. Then the pirate ship came along, the Danish ship engaged it in battle, and he was the only one who managed to get aboard the pirate ship, and he would be able to persuade the pirates to bring him back to Denmark.

In other words, a series of accidents occurred having to do with the letter, his ability to forge the seal, and the pirates. In that series of accidents, Hamlet finds the design of God; "even in that was heaven ordinant." Such a series of chances, clearly undirected by any human choice, any human plan, delivering him from a murder plot that he hadn't expected and returning him to Denmark, where he still had work to do, still had to confront the King, must indicate God's providence. Therefore, he believes, God governs all events. "We defy augury," he says to Horatio; "there is special providence in the fall of a sparrow. If it be not now, 'tis to come; if it be not to come, it will be now; if it be not now, yet it will come: the readiness is all. Since no man of aught he leaves knows, what is to leave betimes? Let be."

We don't know when we're going to die; we do know that we will die. If it's now, okay; it won't come in the future, I don't have to fear about it in the future. If it isn't now, then I don't need to worry about what's happening now. It will come. Since we don't know enough about the world really to understand it, what does it matter if we leave? Let be. Hamlet stops trying to control everything. That is one thing he'd been trying to do with all those intellectual explanations, control everything. Now, he says, let's leave it up to providence. There's a special providence, even in so small a thing as the fall of a sparrow. He's quoting, of course, the Gospel according to Matthew. "Are not two sparrows sold for a farthing? And one of them shall not fall upon the ground without your Father. ... Fear ye not, ye are of much more value than sparrows." God governs all events. Therefore, we do not need to seek explanations in such things as the theory of tragic flaw, according to Aristotle; the theory of fortune, according to Boethius; or even in the theory, according to Isaiah, that God occasionally selects human agents as scourges and ministers. God governs everything; it's not a matter of occasional intervention. God provides all the opportunities. Hamlet need do nothing to set up the circumstances for his final revenge on Claudius.

It happens that Claudius and Laertes have already worked out the whole plot about the duel and the poison. All Hamlet needs to do is take the opportunity when it presents itself. The readiness is all.

He is ready. Horatio expresses the fear that Hamlet will lose that duel to Laertes; Laertes is a notable swordsman. Hamlet says no, don't worry about that, he has been in continual practice since he went into France. He's kept up his swordsmanship; he's in good shape. He can take up the opportunity when it offers itself. In the final scene, in a wonderful display of physical dexterity, moral perception, and intellectual grasping the point, he dominates the scene, defeats Laertes, kills the king,even in the act of killing others, and everything is plain to the audience around them. Everything is made known. He is ready, and the readiness is all.

The tragedy of *Hamlet, Prince of Denmark* is the drama of the Protestant conscience, led into doubt by the puzzlements of the world and the self, trying to amend that doubt with all the learning that antiquity and humanism can make available, and arriving heroically at his own convictions and then acting on them.

Lecture Twenty-Eight
Othello: The Design of the Tragedy

Scope:

Just as Shakespeare's comedies are different one from the other (while sharing certain generic qualities), so too his tragedies vary in their issues and characterizations. *Othello* provides an excellent example to explore this premise, because it is different in so many ways from the other great tragedies. In fact, there is some basis for considering *Othello* to be two plays in one: a romantic comedy in the beginning and a tragedy at the end. None of the other three plays under consideration could be considered as such. We see Shakespeare at work here with his usual abundant genius, transforming genre to achieve dramatic effect.

Outline

I. *Othello* achieves its unique effect in ways different from the other Shakespearean tragedies.

    A. *Othello* lacks the sense of large metaphysical forces: the ghost of *Hamlet*, the supernatural prophecies of *Macbeth*, the frequent speculations about the gods that occur in *King Lear*.

    B. *Othello* deals more with private life than do the other tragedies. In *Romeo and Juliet*, the death of the lovers has a direct impact on the civil order of a city, Verona; in *Hamlet, Macbeth,* and *King Lear*, the welfare of kingdoms is at stake. Although *Othello* begins with great historical conflict between the Christian state of Venice and the Muslim empire of the Turks, that issue evaporates before the end of Act 2.

    C. The value of the play depends on characterization, psychology, psychic interplay, and plot construction.

    D. The design of the play places the tragic deed in a different location.

        1. In *Hamlet, Macbeth,* and *King Lear*, fatal events happen early and the characters must reflect on them.

        2. In *Othello*, nothing fatal occurs until the last act. Thus the characters have little time to reflect; they can only express their shock and horror.

        3. They are helpless to do anything about it or explain it.

    E. The tragic facts prove to be utterly destructive.

1. In Othello, the stakes are lower—only the lives and happiness and commitment of the central couple—but those are altogether annihilated.
2. Unlike the central characters of the other tragedies, Othello and Desdemona are degraded as well as destroyed.

II. In order to create the tragic effects of the play, Shakespeare must first lead the audience to feel the value and preciousness of the love between Desdemona and Othello.

   A. The first two acts of the play constitute a romantic comedy.
      1. Shakespearean comedy assumes that romantic love between a man and a woman is good, natural, irrational in its choices, justifies temporary indecorum, and leads to marriage.
      2. In *Othello*, the lovers are an unlikely pair, differing in age, race, background, and experience. They are also already married.
      3. They encounter the usual obstacles of comedy: a crotchety father, Brabantio; a ridiculous rival lover, Roderigo; and a villain, Iago.
      4. Their situation is investigated and blessed by a good duke, and nature itself appears to cooperate in blessing their union.

   B. In the first scenes, Othello and Desdemona survive vilification.
      1. These two characters are introduced in a bad light (cf., the Iago-Roderigo scene opening Act I).
      2. Iago describes Othello as repulsive in character, appearance, and behavior.
      3. But when he appears, Othello speaks and behaves in a way that demonstrates the descriptions to be almost wholly false.
      4. Brabantio describes his daughter as a shy girl who has been bewitched, but Desdemona proves to be a self-possessed young woman who deliberately chose Othello as her mate.

   C. Although there is no literal wedding scene, the arrival and reunion of Othello and Desdemona on Cyprus after the sea voyage constitutes an equivalent celebration.

1. Iago plays the role of the cynic who cracks dirty jokes at weddings.
2. Cassio's speeches constitute an *epithalamium*, a wedding song celebrating the lovers and their union.

Essential Reading:

Shakespeare, *Othello*.

Supplementary Reading/Viewing:

See video with Olivier.

Sanders, Introduction to *Othello* (New Cambridge edition).

Questions to Consider:

1. Compare Othello and Desdemona with Romeo and Juliet as central characters in a tragi-comedy involving lovers in terms of the "public violence, private bliss" model of Lecture Twenty.

2. A recent version of *Othello* reversed the race of the two central characters, with a white Othello and black Desdemona. What differences might this make in audience perception or reaction to the fatal working out of the plot? Is the theme of the play general enough to admit of still other character reversals based on age, gender, or some other factor? Or would this just ruin an excellent drama? Do you think that we, as late 20th-century viewers, are able to overcome our own biases on some of these issues in order to appreciate the play in an alternative version?

Lecture Twenty-Eight—Transcript
Othello: The Design of the Tragedy

In a famous and influential book of criticism, *Shakespearean Tragedy*, A.C. Bradley announced in 1904 that the great Shakespearean tragedies were four: *Hamlet*, *Othello*, *King Lear*, and *Macbeth*. The quartet has stuck with us as the top of Shakespearean tragedy. Yet, even as he wrote that book, Bradley acknowledged that *Othello* was slightly different from the other three. *Othello* lacked the sense of huge natural or supernatural forces at work—what *Hamlet* does in the way of discovering Providence; what *Macbeth* has in the way of witches and a sense of evil; the persistent questioning in *King Lear* about the nature of the gods. *Othello* operates on a scale closer to ordinary private life than do *Hamlet*, *Macbeth* and *King Lear*. It does not involve the fate of kingdoms. Obviously something is rotten in the whole state of Denmark in *Hamlet*; *Macbeth* concerns all of Scotland; *King Lear* concerns Britain and the universe as a whole. Even *Romeo and Juliet* involves the fate of Verona as a city. With *Othello*, we do not have that sense.

We could have had that sense; *Othello* begins with the great threat of the Turkish Empire to the Venetian Empire, and the Turks and the Venetians did divide the Mediterranean between them in the sixteenth century. We begin with the Senate and the Duke of Venice, a midnight meeting of the Senate in order to determine how to meet the Turkish threat. For people of Shakespeare's time, the Turkish threat was enormous. The Turks had occupied not only the Eastern Mediterranean and what had been the Byzantine Empire, but all of the Balkans. They had been turned back only at the gates of Vienna; and a major sea battle in 1571, when Shakespeare was a child, the Battle of Lepanto, had saved the western Mediterranean from invasion by the Turkish fleet. All that is of concern in the first and second act of *Othello*, but it all drops away. The value of the play lies in the individuality of the characters, the richness of their psychology, their psychic interplay, the clarity and concentration of the plot. It is the closest that Shakespeare wrote to domestic tragedy.

There is a reason for this particular concentration, not only in the scope of the plot, but also in the structure of the play, how the action has been spread out over the five acts. Much that happens in *Othello* depends on the location of what you might call the tragic deed, that act that disrupts nature, disrupts the order of society and causes other bad things to happen in its wake. For Hamlet, that act had happened before the play began, in Claudius' murder of his brother. In *Macbeth*, that act happens quite early in the play, in Act II, when Macbeth murders King Duncan. In *King Lear*, it happens in Act I, when King Lear rejects his daughter's love and wrongly divides his kingdom. In *Othello*, it happens the other way around. Nothing fatal, nothing irrevocable, nothing absolutely dreadful occurs until the very last scene of the play.

The play has a sense of claustrophobia about it. You may feel that something dreadful is going to happen, but none of the characters knows that anything dreadful has happened until the very end. Othello's mind is corrupted by Iago, but we keep thinking that could be reversed. He could find out the truth; he hasn't done anything fatal in his state of delusion. It isn't until he murders Desdemona in the last scene that something fatal is done. Then it is so late that the characters have almost no time to reflect upon it. All they can do is respond in horror. It is characteristic of the last scene in *Othello* that we do not get big statements about the meaning of suffering. We just get exclamations about how terrible it is. "O monstrous act!" "O villainy!" O thou Othello…What shall be said to thee?" Or, in one of the most expressive lines of the whole play, simply "Oh, oh, oh," which I cannot possibly act out of context. Confronted with Othello's murder of his wife Desdemona, the bystanding characters are, in effect, helpless. They merely register the shock of it, or the pity of it. No one can do anything about it, either in a practical way or in an explanatory way. In fact, it is so terrible to them that it almost gives the sense of being obscene.

At the ends of other plays, the bodies are displayed. When Lear's daughters die at the end of *King Lear*, Albany orders the bodies to be produced. When Hamlet dies, Fortinbras says, "Bear Hamlet's body to the stage." These are objects of honor that should be paid attention to. At the end of this play, the character left in charge, Lodovico, says, "This object poisons sight. Let it be hid." This object is the bodies of Desdemona, Othello and Emilia on the bed, the tragic loading of this bed. Moreover, the facts with which we are confronted at the end of the play are utterly distractive ones.

What is threatened in this play is a single thing—the love of Desdemona and Othello, the intense happiness these two have achieved with each other. The welfare of the Venetian state, the order of the universe do not hinge upon the individual happiness of this couple, but the couple themselves absolutely depend upon it. Desdemona is no longer a senator's daughter. She is Othello's "fair warrior." Othello is no longer an independent man. When his love for Desdemona is threatened, he cries, "Othello's occupation's gone." In other words, they have rewritten their own identities in total commitment to each other. It's a play about commitment. Their marriage is the most important thing about them. They have surrendered separate identities to be a couple, and their happiness together is completely and utterly destroyed by the play, wholly ruined, nothing preserved or rescued.

That is, the stakes may be lower than in *Hamlet* or in *Lear*, but the effect is more intense and more painful, even more painful because they don't only die, they are denigrated. The action of this play abuses Desdemona, and it degrades Othello. If we sympathize with these people, we are unrelievedly appalled at what happens to them. It's an extremely painful play. Therefore, if this is the effect to be achieved, it is of the utmost importance that Shakespeare make us feel the preciousness and value of what Othello and Desdemona have achieved in their love for each other, in their personal happiness before the trouble starts. Shakespeare must thoroughly create, in poetry and in action, the thing that will be destroyed, before setting about the tragic process of destroying it.

Again, look at the design of the tragedy. The tragic deed, the smothering of Desdemona, does not take place until the final scene. The tragic process, the corruption of Othello's mind to get him to the point where he will kill his wife, doesn't begin until the middle of the play, until Act III. Not, in fact, until the end of Act II, does Iago arrive at any kind of coherent plan about how he will work on Othello. Not until Act III, Scene 3, does he begin actually to put it into motion. Instead, the opening half of the play is devoted to action that establishes positive values. The first two acts of the play, in fact, constitute a romantic comedy. *Othello* is a tragedy built on a comedy, and the comedy is given to us with great fullness. Hamlet may start his play already dressed in black, and Macbeth may enter his play with murder already in his heart, but Othello and Desdemona start off as lovers. In Shakespeare, love is a wonderful thing. Love is right, and what is right is natural. The lovers in comedy are in tune with the forces of nature, the forces that renew life. The naturalness of love often provides the warrant for lovers to sweep aside ordinary inhibitions, normal proprieties of behavior, restrictions put upon people by decorum in society, they move toward some fulfilling environment.

In the actual comedies, they move out into a green world—into the forest of Arden, into the wood outside Athens. Good dukes and good princes eventually bless and validate their love and sweep aside whatever law or other obstacle stands in their path. In the comedies, natural and uninhibited love is also sometimes irrational in its choice of object. Whom we love is often beyond our control and often a person whom our parents or other relatives think is unlikely, inappropriate. It's a spontaneous and instinctive matter. Most of the comedies, after all, do depend on love at first sight. Very frequently, Daddy says, "No, I want you to marry somebody else." This produces ludicrous situations and temporary conflicts, but the conflicts are resolved, the situations cease to be ludicrous, and the choice of love is ratified. Comedies end with marriage, either promised and forthcoming, or marriage actually celebrated by some sort of ceremony on the stage. Marriage celebrates the rightness, the naturalness, the goodness of love.

Marriage is considered to be the completion that crowns the story of lovers. Thus, Shakespearean comedy places all the stresses that happen in a sexual relationship in the courtship period, before the actual wedding. It is silent about significant problems or changes of direction that may befall people who are already married to each other. It implies the fairytale formula; they live happily ever after. I'm not saying that Shakespeare, or the Elizabethans in general, were stupid, that they assumed that married people have no difficulties. Of course they knew that married people have difficulties. They'd had this king, Henry VIII, who went through six wives, after all. But the form of comedy does not ordinarily encompass such matters. Here is a way to describe the uniqueness of *Othello*; it deals with a post-comic world. We have the comedy, but it's over by the end of Act II. Then we go on with what can happen in a marriage. It appears to accept the assumptions of comedy, and then it exposes them as containing the roots of tragedy.

In the comedy of the first two acts of *Othello*, we have an unlikely pair of lovers, indeed a pair that no one has thought possible, except they themselves. Everyone around them acts with astonishment. Othello is middle-aged. He is a lifelong bachelor. He has lived a life of action, of wandering and a military career. He is non-urban, he is foreign, and he is black. Desdemona is young; she is the daughter of a great senator, brought up in the expectation of a marriage. She is inexperienced, she is urban, she is native to the society of Venice, and she is white. Onstage, she is almost always blond to heighten the contrast. We have the usual barrier figures: the blocking father, her father, the senator Brabantio, who is outraged, accuses Othello of having used charms and other medicines to bring about Desdemona's affection for him. There is also a disappointed rival, Roderigo, who tries to set up obstacles. There's a villain, Iago, but there is a good duke, and the duke hears the case. The Senate scene, that is, the big scene of Act I, is a kind of trial scene where, for a moment, the pressing business that afflicts the Venetian empire, the fact that the Turks are attacking and presenting a great danger, is set aside. Everybody says, "Let us hear this case about whether Othello properly married Desdemona or not. Let us turn into a domestic court instead of the ruling body of the empire."

It is discovered that this is a good thing. The duke blesses the marriage, and nature herself seems to cooperate in blessing the marriage. The couple immediately has set forth to Cyprus in pursuit of Othello's professional duties. They sail there. They have to go through a terrific storm, but the storm itself goes calm and allows them to arrive at Cyprus, The storm does one thing before it goes calm—it disperses those nasty Turks. Nature herself will take care of the enemy and let through the young lovers—or the young and middle-aged married couple—to their happiness on the island.

I must add one major thing to what Othello and Desdemona go through when this marriage is discovered in the process of Acts I and II. They survive not only storm and tempest, and the investigation of the Senate, the blocking father and the disappointed rival. They survive vilification, misrepresentation, scandalous reports of what they are doing. These characters are introduced in a very bad light, Othello in the worst possible light. The opening conversation in the play is between Iago and Roderigo, who dislike Othello very much. They reveal the wedding, the elopement, to Brabantio, who is not happy about this news at all. Thus, in that opening conversation, long before we see Othello, we get a lot of description of him.

He is described as "loving his own pride and purposes." We're told that he talks in bombast, that he's done something terribly unfair about promoting Cassio over Iago's head, when Iago really deserved the promotion. He's described an "an extravagant and wheeling stranger." They suggest to Brabantio that Othello was really trying to rob him, to steal his wealth as well as his daughter. Brabantio suggests that Desdemona was corrupted by spells. Nastiest of all, the union between Othello and Desdemona is described in physical terms as being very unattractive: "an old black ram / ... tupping your white ewe;" "your daughter is covered with a Barbary horse;" "your daughter / and the Moor are making the beast with two backs." Very unattractive descriptions of sexual intercourse, bestial, disgusting and designed to arouse all latent racial animosities; "your daughter is in bed with a black man."

We may be suspicious of some of these descriptions. We know that Iago dislikes the Moor when he says these kinds of things, but we're not in a position to contradict these descriptions until we see Othello himself. Then, when we see Othello himself, it turns out, he's not like that at all. He's black, but he's not full of bombast. He's not extravagant and wheeling; he's not doing anything physically disgusting to Desdemona. He is very self-controlled; he is almost monosyllabic. He is princely, anything but bestial. He is magnificent. His first line is, "'Tis better as it is." Nothing could be more controlled. When Iago says, "Brabantio's run off to the Senate to complain about you stealing his daughter, and he's raising the utmost fuss," Othello says, "Let him do his spite. / My services, which I have done the signiory, / Shall out-tongue his complaints." He's perfectly self-confident of himself and of his position in Venice.

When Iago suggests, "Perhaps you'd better go back inside the inn and not be found here in the street. This might be a messy encounter," Othello says, "No, I must be found." It would be ridiculous if the general were hiding indoors when there is disorder in the streets. Othello is able to quell it with a single line: "Put up your bright swords, for the dew will rust them." He doesn't need to get out his own sword. It's just one line that cuts across the bright swords of the quarrelers in the street.

The courtship has been unusual, has been romantic. We are given a description of how Othello wooed her, unintentionally, simply telling the story of his life, telling it without egotism, telling it with no emphasis on what he'd achieved, simply about the interesting places he has been.

> Of moving accidents by flood and field,
>
> Of hair-breadth escapes in the imminent deadly breach,
>
> Of being taken by the insolent foe
>
> And sold to slavery, of my redemption thence
>
> And portage in my travel history;
>
> Whereof of antres vast and deserts idle,
>
> Rough quarries, rocks, and hills whose heads touch heaven,
>
> It was my hint to speak—

Sounds like there was more emphasis on the geography than what happened to him.

There is a similar bit of misleading having to do with Desdemona, with the heroine. We don't see her, either, and she is described by Brabantio as being shy and reclusive, blushing, "a maiden never bold, / Of spirit so still and quiet that her motion / Blush'd at herself." Sounds like a perfect little ninny. Actually, this girl who's supposed to be so shy and never bold, stands up in the middle of the Senate at midnight and defends herself as having chosen her own husband, with self-possession, rationality and grace. She says, "I owe you duty, Father. You begot me, you bred me, you raised me. But now I owe my lord Othello duty. So much duty as my mother owed you, I owe Othello." It's perfectly self-possessed, firm. It is neither scared nor gushy. She is not saying, "But Daddy, I love him." She knows exactly where she is. These are people in control of their own destinies.

The final step in this two-act comedy of love is that the love is celebrated. It is given a full-throated, gloriously poetic celebration when they arrive in Cyprus. There is no wedding scene proper in this play. We do not see an actual marriage being celebrated. What we see is a carefully orchestrated procession, whereby the people having to do with this wedding arrive on Cyprus, upon the island of Venus. Cyprus is sacred to Venus; it is the island of love. Shakespeare is most careful to arrange it. There are three ships bringing the Venetians to Cyprus. On the first comes Cassio. On the second come Desdemona, brought by Iago, and Iago's wife Emilia. On the third arrives Othello, so that we have a carefully graduated procession coming, with each group worried about how safe the group coming after them are, because there are still the tail ends of that storm around. This, as I say, is orchestrated as a kind of wedding scene.

Othello and Desdemona are, of course, the bridal pair, and Emilia is attending on Desdemona as a kind of lady-in-waiting or matron of honor. Cassio is the best man. Cassio is the one who gets to say all the good things about how wonderful a couple these are, to make, as it were, the toast. Iago is the guy there always is at the wedding, the guy who's over in the corner making dirty jokes about what's really been going on. "Do you suppose she's pregnant? How long have they really known each other? Is this going to be any good?" There's always that cynic at a wedding, usually sitting at the bar drinking too much. But it's Cassio as celebrator, as best man, that particularly interests me. He is singing what is called, in sixteenth-century poetry, an epithalamium, a marriage-song. Montano, who is on the island of Cyprus, who is the temporary governor there, asks him, "Good lieutenant, is your general wived?" Cassio answers, "Most fortunately"—with the greatest of good fortune, he is wived.

> He hath achieved a maid
> That paragons description and wild fame,
> One that excels the quirks of blazoning pens,
> And in the essential vesture of creation
> Does tire the ingener.

This woman is so beautiful, she cannot be described by a pen, by a poet who would write about how beautiful this bride is. In the essential vesture of creation, she would tire the ingener, the ingenious poet. My text, the Bevington text, has a note on that, saying, "In her real beauty, she would outdo anyone who would inventively praise her." But, I think, "the essential vesture of creation" is more than "in her beauty." The essential vesture of creation is, of course, nudity. God created Eve naked. We came into the world naked. It would tire the ingenious poet to describe her in her naked glory. She is as naked as Eve or, perhaps more relevantly, as naked as the goddess Venus. This is her island; she is coming to shore on it. She is like Botticelli's Venus being blown ashore on Cyprus, washed ashore in the Mediterranean island, Venus risen from the waves, Venus Anadyomene. In fact, she is "divine Desdemona" in Cassio's next speech:

> The gutter'd rocks, and congregated sands—

> Traitors ensteep'd to clog the guiltless keel,—
>
> As having sense of beauty, do omit
>
> Their mortal natures, letting go safely by
>
> The divine Desdemona.

She's "our great captain's captain," not only Venus Anadyomene, but Venus Armata, Venus armed.

> The riches of the ship is come on shore!
>
> Ye men of Cyprus, let her have your knees.
>
> Hall to thee, lady! And the grace of heaven,
>
> Before, behind thee, and on every hand,
>
> Enwheel thee round!

The grace of heaven on all sides of her: Venus Anadyomene, Venus Armata, the Venus of Botticelli's "Primavera," who has the graces of heaven around her, the three graces. Or perhaps even the Virgin Mary herself, and wheeled around by stars. Cassio is calling upon all these associations for this marvelous wedding poem, extolling the bride as a goddess. Othello, too, is a god worth her. He is the Mars who will marry this Venus, and who comes to her, claiming her to be "O my fair warrior." She responds, "My dear Othello," and he goes on:

> It gives me wonder great as my content
>
> To see you here before me. O my soul's joy!
>
> If after every tempest come such calms,
>
> May the winds blow till they have waken'd death!
>
> And let the laboring bark climb hills of seas
>
> Olympus-high, and duck again as low
>
> As hell's from heaven! If it were now to die,
>
> 'Twere now to be most happy.

He is so delighted, he can scarcely believe this is happening—that moment of joy when you reach out toward the person you love, and she reaches back. You can scarcely believe that the love is reciprocal, that you are together. This is a union totally celebrated, totally given to us, totally given to each other. The play depends on getting that established first.

Lecture Twenty-Nine
Othello: "O Villainy!"

Scope:

As mentioned in the last lecture, and as suggested by the title, the role of Iago is a central one to this play. His villainy is somewhat hard to handle, since his motive is hard to pin down, and Shakespeare doesn't really give us any help at the shocking end of the play. This lecture will advance some of the theories put forth to explain Iago and lead us to consider the nature of evil.

Outline

I. Iago proposes to destroy the happiness achieved by Othello and Desdemona. Why he does this is problematic.

    A. He adduces some five motives for his schemes, but they are not dwelt upon consistently:

        1. Othello has deprived him of a promotion in favor of Cassio.

        2. Othello has possibly cuckolded Iago.

        3. He fears that Cassio has also cuckolded him.

        4. He seems to admit a desire for Desdemona, but this is not really clear.

        5. He admits that Cassio makes him feel ugly

    B. In the final scene Shakespeare ostentatiously refuses to explain Iago.

    C. As critic Bernard Spivack points out, Iago may be a Renaissance embodiment of a character from medieval drama, the Vice of the morality play, a tempter who takes pleasure in deceit for its own sake and has a special relationship with the audience.

        1. Is Iago a "demi-devil?" He uses much language and imagery of Hell and the devil.

        2. In the final act, Othello looks at Iago's feet, expecting to see cloven hooves.

    D. Modern psychoanalysis suggests that Iago is motivated by repressed homosexuality: he destroys Othello and Cassio because he resents their attractiveness to him, displacing his love for them onto Desdemona, and then punishing her for it.

<ol style="list-style-type: decimal">
<li>The language with which he describes Cassio suggests sexual desire.</li>
<li>The poisoning of Othello's mind is a seduction climaxing in a quasi-marital vow.</li>
</ol>

II. The Vice theory and the psychoanalytic theory are abstractions. Neither catches the full experience of Iago's hatred.

    A. Shakespeare's business as a dramatist is to capture the texture of living, not the explanations people offer in intellectual analysis.

    B. Promiscuous hatred and envy do exist. In this case, they transcend any specific motives Iago offers for his actions.

    C. Shakespeare allows his characters to probe the meaning of their suffering.

        1. In the case of Iago, this involves probing why he is inflicting suffering on other people.

        2. As Coleridge said, Iago is "the motive-hunting of motiveless malignity."

III. Iago believes that the secret of life lies in self-knowledge, self-love, and self-control. This is well illustrated in his dialogue with Roderigo in the last sixty lines of Act 1 Scene 2.

    A. The view has sound Elizabethan basis but omits any suggestion of spiritual life or grace. His language in many passages debases human life.

        1. He places his emphasis on his own will.

        2. He denies any spiritual operation in such relationships as love, heroism, or self-sacrifice.

        3. He denies everything that makes a human being anything other than a calculating animal.

    B. Iago is envious of those who live more idealistically.

        1. Iago really does possess an irrational hatred and envy.

        2. He therefore tries to "enmesh them all."

        3. He is really entirely self-centered and cannot stand others who are not.

Essential Reading:

Shakespeare, *Othello*.

Questions to Consider:

1. Evaluate the five possible motives given in paragraph I.A. that might have impelled Iago to carry out his actions. Are any or all of them compelling?

2. Have we encountered any other villains like Iago elsewhere in Shakespeare? If so, where? Support your conclusion with specific examples of the behavior and psychology of the other character(s).

Lecture Twenty-Nine—Transcript
Othello: "O Villainy!"

I ended the last lecture with an ecstatic account of the marital happiness of Othello and Desdemona as they arrived on the island of Cyprus. There is one detail to be added to that account. During that full-throated epithalamium, Iago is standing always on the side of the stage. At the end of it, he says quietly, "O you are well tuned now! / But I'll set down the pegs that tune that music." Iago proposes to destroy their happiness, to destroy the music, which always a symbol of harmony in Shakespeare, to produce discords on the pegs. Why?

Iago is one of the big problems in Shakespearean criticism. There has been much throwing about of brains as to why Iago chooses to destroy Othello, Desdemona, Cassio, Roderigo, the rest of them. Why does he do the terrible things he does? He does acknowledge some motives. He soliloquizes to us frequently and mentions some five or six reasons why he should be doing this. First, that Othello has deprived him of a post that he felt he deserved. He should have promoted Iago to be his lieutenant. Instead, he passed Iago over and appointed Michael Cassio. That sounds quite legitimate when first we are introduced to the motive. The trouble is, he forgets that after a while, and we begin to get other motives. That, for example, Othello has cuckolded Iago, slept with his wife Emilia. Then he mentions later on that he "fears Cassio with his night-cap too," that Cassio may have cuckolded him with Emilia. There's one passage in which he seems to admit a desire for Desdemona himself. That's not quite clear; that's why I had to say five or six motives. It certainly is the motive for Iago in the source story, the Italian tale by Cintio that Shakespeare was adapting. But it's not quite clear that it carries over. He does admit that there is "a daily beauty" in Cassio's life that makes him feel ugly. Finally, he says that he wants to "plume up [his] will / In double knavery," whatever that means—just to enjoy being wicked?

The difficulty with this is, of course, there are too many motives, and none of them are dwelt upon with the kind of insistence that would really make them convincing. When a man in Shakespeare is jealous of his wife, we hear about it at great length, not just a passing, "I fear Cassio with my night-cap." When a man is ambitious, when a man is disappointed, Shakespeare writes long speeches about these things. These motives are tossed off and left to dangle as they may.

At the end of the play, Shakespeare apparently refuses to explain Iago altogether. All the characters onstage want to know why Iago has done what he's done, once it is revealed in the final scene what he has done. In particular, Othello says, "demand that demi-devil / Why he hath thus ensnared my soul and body?" Iago replies, "Demand me nothing; what you know, you know. / From this time forth I never will speak word." Indeed, he never does; he has no further lines in the play. Iago declines to explain himself to others. He declines to open his motives to them, or to us. Perhaps there's a clue in one word that Othello just used—"demand that demi-devil / Why." Is Iago a demi-devil?

It has been argued, with some frequency, that Iago embodies an abstract form of evil that is derived from the older allegorical drama of the Middle Ages. The primary statement of this lies in a book called *Shakespeare and the Allegory of Evil*, written by a distinguished scholar called Bernard Spivack. He argues that the figure of Iago is based on the medieval character of the Vice. The medieval drama put in the center of the stage an Everyman figure, a mankind figure, representative of us all; put on opposite sides of him Virtues, showing him the steep and thorny path to Heaven, and Vices, inviting him down the primrose path of dalliance to Hell. The Vice figure was the most popular character in the English medieval drama, the one whom the audience most loved.

The Vice, with a capital V, posed as being a friend of his victim, devoted to the welfare of mankind. He also gloried in his deceit. He practiced seduction as a sport, he developed a special relationship with the audience because he did a lot of soliloquizing—"Look how I'm going to seduce this foolish young man into sinfulness." He is, in fact, a stage-manager of the action, put onstage to control it. In this medieval drama, Vice seduces Everyman without any real personal motive for it, simply in fulfillment of his nature as a Vice. The Vice is a tempter, simply as it is a function of the Statue of Liberty to hold up the torch of freedom, an allegorical person. In this view, in Spivack's argument, the core of Iago is this old medieval tempter. The few human motives that are mentioned by Iago in the course of *Othello* are just put on to put a few scraps of clothing onto the bare allegorical bones.

This is a good argument; there is much reason to associate Iago with such a figure. Iago frequently invokes Hell during the course of

Shakespeare's play. At the end of Act I, he begins to have an idea of what scheme he will practice on Othello, and he says in soliloquy, "I have't. It is engender'd. Hell and night / Must bring this monstrous birth to the world's light." At the end of Act II, when he has developed the plan further, he has a soliloquy beginning: "Divinity of hell"— theology of Hell, I am working out of the arguments of Hell—

> When devils will the blackest sins put on,
>
> They do suggest at first with heavenly shows,
>
> As I do now.

"I am behaving like a devil." The imagery of Hell and devils frequently surrounds Iago long before Othello calls him a demi-devil at the end of the play. It climaxes at the end of the play with that demi-devil line and one other very revealing line of Othello's, "I look down at his feet, but that's a fable." He's looking down at Iago's feet expecting to see a cloven hoof, expecting to see the Devil's foot.

There is a great deal to all this. The scholars who've explored the medieval background of Shakespearean drama have performed a valuable service in explaining the ancestry of Shakespeare's practices, explaining the concepts and patterns which the drama had been previously using, and which were therefore readily available to Shakespeare and his fellow playwrights, readily comprehensible to his audience. Any playwright in any period needs such a collection of concepts or forms to dramatize his stories with. That doesn't mean he needs to stick to them; it doesn't mean he can only deploy the same old stereotypes. But to achieve communication, you need to have some common ground. A playwright needs both originality and old stuff. He needs stereotypes before he can start remolding them into something that's appropriate to his particular purpose at the moment that he's writing this play. I think this is relevant.

Let me pause here and go on to a different kind of explanation. On the other hand, we need not run full tilt into the medieval past to explain Iago and say, "Iago is only a relic of the Middle Ages." There are modern explanations too. If the medievals had their concepts, schemes and allegories, so do we also in the twentieth century. The chief inventors of patterns and concepts that describe and explain human behavior in the twentieth century are the psychologists. Modern specialists see men in a psychic pattern, caught in the toils of the unconscious. In particular, several psychoanalysts have produced brilliant readings of Iago as motivated by unconscious, repressed homosexuality.

This argument goes as follows: he is in love with Othello, and in love with Cassio, or at least attracted to them both. They are both highly attractive men. He cannot permit himself to recognize this fact, so he proceeds to cope with it by a variety of unconscious strategies. So far, there certainly seems to be something to this; he's fascinated with both Cassio and Othello. He pays them much more attention than he pays his own wife. The strategy is to destroy the objects of his love. They pose a threat to him. If he ever has to face what he really feels about them, that will ruin him. He's terribly resentful of them, so he wants to ruin them first. That is, he's going to displace or reject his love for them by foisting it on Desdemona, saying, "I don't desire Cassio, I don't desire Othello. She does. Therefore, let us punish them all for being involved in these wicked desires."

There is much to this; you can find support in the lines of the play. I quoted a moment ago, the line saying "There is a daily beauty in [Cassio's] life / That makes me ugly." That's a point where his admiration of Cassio seems to surface in the spoken script and not just be subtext. There's something even more revealing when he's tempting Othello into believing that Cassio has slept with Desdemona. He invents a dream that he reports Cassio as having had. He and Cassio spent the night together, shared quarters one night. He, Iago,

> being troubled with a raging tooth,
>
> I could not sleep.
>
> There are a kind of men so loose of soul,
>
> That in their sleeps will mutter their affairs;
>
> One of this kind is Cassio.
>
> In sleep I heard him say, 'Sweet Desdemona,
>
> Let us be wary, let us hide our loves'—

Cassio babbled in his sleep about being in love with Desdemona. That's OK, but look where it goes from there:

> And then, sir, would he gripe and wring my hand,

And cry, 'Sweet creature!' and then kiss me hard,

As if he pluck'd up kisses by the roots,

That grew upon my lips; then laid his leg

Over my thigh, and sigh'd and kiss'd; and then

Cried, 'Cursed fate that gave thee to the Moor!'

Iago is playing out a fantasy of Cassio making love to him. It's a pretty hot fantasy too. The whole point is to inflame Othello, but it may tell us more about what's going on in Iago's mind, in the lower reaches. That would suggest a relation with Cassio, the desire for Cassio. The desire for Othello is there in the whole temptation of Othello into jealousy of Desdemona. The deception of Othello is played as a very long step-by-step scene in the middle of the play. It is, in fact, a seduction scene, as Iago gets closer and closer to the personal affairs of Othello. It ends with their swearing a vow to each other. Iago kneels onstage and says:

Witness, you ever-burning lights above,

You elements that clip us round about,

Witness that here Iago doth give up

The execution of his wit, hands, heart,

To wrong'd Othello's service!

Othello replies, "I greet thy love, / Not with vain thanks, but with acceptance bounteous.… Now art thou my lieutenant." Iago replies, "I am your own forever." The two of them are kneeling onstage swearing this vow of eternal loyalty. It is almost a marriage scene, a wedding scene. It carries that impact.

This is a possible modern interpretation of Iago's motivations, and it has been used in modern productions by no less a person than Laurence Olivier. Laurence Olivier had already played a Freudian Hamlet. When he went on to play Iago opposite the Othello of Ralph Richardson, he called up Ernest Jones, the disciple of Freud, from whom he got the Freudian ideas about Hamlet, and said, "Can you give me some Freudian ideas about Iago too?" What I have just explained is what he got, and Olivier worked that out into the staging. Richardson, playing Othello, didn't really understand what he was doing. Richardson didn't go in for this kind of thing at all. There is a famous moment where, in rehearsal, Olivier kissed

Richardson on the mouth, and Richardson said, "Dear boy, dear boy, this will never do."

As a matter of fact, the idea did not, in fact, do. This took place in 1937. Freudian ideas were not very widespread in England at that time. The audience didn't understand what was going on. If you read the critics reviewing that production, you will see that they didn't understand. Nonetheless, it's a possible idea, and I have no objection to an actor's preparing a role in this kind of deft, psychological way. I've no real objection to Freudian analysis as a sort of intellectual exercise. There is a problem here, that you are working on the play as if it were a case history. You can't actually put Iago on the couch and ask him to free-associate, and do the sort of Freudian analysis that you would with a live patient.

Both the medieval vice theory and the psychoanalytic repressed homosexual theory resort to abstract patterns to find a context for some rather mysterious behavior. I want to put these two ideas together, the medieval idea and the twentieth century idea. They really are both abstractions for behavior that we find painful to acknowledge. It is really we who need an explanation for hatred, for Iago's lust to destroy others. I think the Freudian idea is as much an allegory as the medieval idea. Both of them tend to flatten out the tortured humanity of Iago. Promiscuous hatred of the kind exemplified in Iago does exist in human life. It disturbs us deeply; we ache to know why it should exist. To know why might help us deal with the pain. It might perhaps help us know what to do if we encountered a person as consumed with hatred as Iago is. You notice we do this with unpleasant feelings. If there is someone who is bountiful, loving, generous to all mankind, we don't ask what peculiar complex in that person makes him so forthcoming. We do it with evil and disturbing things.

Actually, I don't think Shakespeare has to supply us with an explanation. He supplies us with the experience. That's his business as a playwright, to show us what hatred and envy are like, hatred and envy and destructiveness. He recognizes that we want explanations. He has Othello ask at the end of the play, "Why has he ensnared my soul and body?" Even more, he has Iago ask. He has Iago offer up those six motives that I listed at the beginning, as if he himself were trying to figure out why he is so hateful. I've been saying throughout these lectures on tragedy that Shakespeare does not have an all-encompassing explanation of the meaning of tragedy; rather, that he allows the characters to probe the meaning of their suffering.

It is part of the tragic experience that he writes that the characters themselves are perplexed by it. It is part of the suffering that they go through an effort to find explanations, that they try to account for it to themselves. In this particular case, in the case of Iago, we find a man asking not why he's suffering, but why is he inflicting suffering on other people. I think the hatred is greater than any explanation we can offer for it, any explanation that Iago can offer for it. A very famous phrase has been applied to it by the early nineteenth-century poet and critic Samuel Taylor Coleridge. Coleridge described Iago's favorite activity as "the motive-hunting of motiveless malignity." He is malign; it is without a motive, and he himself hunts for the motive. I think that phrase captures something essentially accurate about Iago; the malignity does transcend the motive. Iago desires to do dirt on life. That, by the way, was D.H. Lawrence's phrase for it. To blacken what is true, good or beautiful, or to use Iago's own phrase, "to turn their virtue into pitch;" that envy of the daily beauty in Cassio's life that makes him ugly. I think he also envies Othello and Desdemona's beauty.

There's a bit in Iago of the homely, chubby, greasy-haired high school boy who isn't popular, and who envies the in-crowd, the school leaders, the athletes and the cheerleaders, and who gets back at them by being cleverer than they are, by entrapping them with his wit. He certainly dislikes anything that they have that is beautiful. Therefore, when he describes the imagined sex between Desdemona and Othello—of course, he hadn't seen them having sex—he describes it in that terrible way, they're "making the beast with two backs. An old black ram is tupping your white ewe." He likes starting brawls; he likes starting fights. He starts a riot in the first scene of the play with Brabantio's servants. He gets Cassio drunk in the second act, and that turns into a sword fight. There's a third brawl in the streets in the last act, which results in Roderigo's death and the wounding of Cassio.

The man is possessed by an irrational hatred. He desires, again in his phrase, "to enmesh them all." What's really strongest in the writing of Iago is not the explanations offered, but the verbs describing the activity: "to turn virtue into pitch," "to enmesh them all." He despises most of the rest of mankind. He despises any man who does not keep his heart strictly attending on himself, any man who fails to be guided by self-interest. Yet it irritates him enormously that, in this preposterous world, men and women who do have instincts of generosity and regard for honor and honesty, such as Desdemona, Othello, Cassio, somehow manage to be thought well of, even are successful.

They are successful; in Othello's case, they are also powerful, noble, generous, true and imaginative. Iago just can't bear that. He's got his own doctrine of life, which is entirely self-centered. Shakespeare gives him a complete set of beliefs about how human beings should really behave. This comes at the end of the Senate scene. He's talking to Roderigo alone, after everyone else has left the stage, the end of Act I, Scene III. Roderigo mentions virtue. Iago responds:

> Virtue? a fig! 'Tis in ourselves that we are thus or thus. Our bodies are our gardens, to the which our wills are gardeners; so that if we will plant nettles, or sow lettuce, set hyssop and weed up thyme, … why, the power and corrigible authority of this lies in our wills.

That is, we can do what we want with ourselves, make ourselves full of nettles, or make ourselves full of lettuce. To go back to quoting him:

> If the balance of our lives had not one scale of reason to poise another of sensuality, the blood and baseness of our natures would conduct us to most preposterous conclusions. We have reason to cool our raging motions, our carnal stings, our unbitted lusts; whereof I take this, that you call love, to be a sect or scion.

Love is merely a lust of the blood and a permission of the will. We are completely in control. We are gardeners to the garden of our bodies. Our wills can do what we want; our wills can control our passions. Love is just a passion, a lust of the blood, seconded by a permission of the will. This is sound Elizabethan psychology. They did believe that the reason should control the passions, that we were given our wills to exert that control, that we were full of lusts left over from the Fall of Adam from our corrupted natural condition, but that the will and the reason should control our desires in this fashion. This doctrine, in other words, that Iago is preaching to Roderigo, has enough truth in it to be plausible, in fact a great deal of truth. What's wrong with it is simply what is left out.

Iago supposes that the individual human will is all-powerful. He does not admit the existence of any other power, that there might be anything like grace in the world, God's power, God's gift to strengthen us in our overcoming our baser desires, God's mercy, God's forgiveness. He denies implicitly, in this description of our psychology, any spiritual operation, that love is anything more than a lust of the blood and a permission of the will, that love might be a genuine attraction toward another person, finding in that other person something comparable to ourselves, finding in that other person beauty, finding in that other person an image of God. He denies implicitly any sort of imagination that sees beyond ourselves as fleshly creatures. He denies any heroism, any self-sacrifice. He denies all those things that make us more than calculating animals.

Iago's viewpoint in human beings is really rather simple. It is also rather brutal, and I mean that literally—animalistic, of the brutes— and finally rather dull in the way he limits the possibilities of humankind. His effect on other people is malignant; his effect on the audience can be mesmerizing. For a while, we follow this man as he exerts his great cleverness, his cynicism, his resourcefulness. We even may be amused by him as he plays tricks on other people, until we realize how empty, narrow and destructive it is, how much it hurts other people whom we, in fact, like much more, other people who have possibilities for heroism, love, and self-sacrifice.

Lecture Thirty
Othello: "The Noble Moor"

Scope:

As we discussed in Lecture 28, *Othello* is different from the other great tragedies in many ways. Therefore, it is not surprising that the lead character is also different from the other tragic protagonists. In this lecture, we will first compare Othello with Hamlet to note key differences in character and then consider what negative things critics have said about Othello in an attempt to determine the aptness of his sobriquet of "the noble Moor."

Outline

I.   Othello is a man of action and achievement.

    A. In many ways he is the opposite of Hamlet.

        1. Hamlet is a young university student; Othello, a middle-aged soldier.

        2. Hamlet is European; Othello is African.

        3. Hamlet is a failure at love; Othello is happily married.

        4. Hamlet is not free, but rather caught in a situation not of his own creation, subject to his birth as a prince and the actions of his parents and his uncle. Othello, although born a prince in Africa, has pursued a career of his own choosing and can show his own accomplishments. He is free.

    B. Early in the play, Othello behaves with unfailing resourcefulness.

        1. In Act 1 Scene 3, he handles Brabantio and the Senate with courteous firmness.

        2. In Act 2 Scene 3, he handles Cassio with both affection and professional judgment.

        3. It is his characteristic action in both Act 1 and Act 2 to quell disorder.

    C. His imposing quality appears in his speech, the "Othello music." The critic G. Wilson Knight has described this stately, brilliant, picturesque, and exotic mode of expression as typified by strong verbs, the imperative mode of address, and imagery, as exemplified by his famous "Pontic sea" speech in Act 3 Scene 3.

D. The heroic authority of this figure is reinforced by his color.

   1. There is the visual importance of blackness on the stage. It makes Othello separate, free, and commanding.

   2. The racial entanglements of blackness are particularly conflicting for modern audiences.

   3. Is Shakespeare saying that Othello is tricked because he is black? If so, then the play is racist.

   4. If Othello thinks he is inferior to the white Europeans around him, we have missed the self-confidence of the character. He has not suffered the dehumanization of subsequent race slavery.

E. A particular mark of his heroism is his capacity for personal commitment: to his profession as warrior and then to his love for Desdemona.

II. This heroic figure suffers unusual degradation.

   A. The degradation is both physical and verbal. In Act 4 Scene 1, he sprawls on the floor in an epileptic fit, and his stately language turns into animalistic spluttering.

   B. Critics degrade him by finding him full of flaws.

   1. Except for Coriolanus, he is the only Shakespearean tragic hero whom people have thought stupid.

   2. In fact, while he may lack Hamlet's intellectual subtlety, he is not stupid.

   3. We may be irritated that he is taken in by Iago's lies.

   4. Unlike other deceptions in Shakespeare, which work quickly, Act 3 Scene 3 of Othello dramatizes this deception in agonizingly extensive detail.

   C. His most serious mistake may be not in believing the lies told by his trusted subaltern, but that he lets them corrupt his mind and emotions. His speech at 3.3.260 shows him moving from love to indifference to murderous vengeance, a transition that happens in other plays with white protagonists.

III. In Act 5, Othello attempts to handle his revenge with the disinterested quality of a judge.

   A. He imagines himself a judge acting merely for "the cause," but his emotions overwhelm this attempted detachment and he kills Desdemona in a rage.

B. He ends the play, as he had started, as a judge and defender of civilization, but now the enemy to be defeated is not the Turks or civil riot, but himself.

C. His suicide is therefore the last act of heroism of the "noble Moor."

Essential Reading:

Shakespeare, *Othello*.

Questions to Consider:

1. Consider the issue of Othello's blackness. Is this metaphor? Is Shakespeare sending a subtle racial message (consider both positive and negative aspects of any such "message")? Is it possible for modern listeners, especially Americans, to view the play unhindered by the realities of racial history occurring after Shakespeare's time?

2. Do you think it is plausible that a character with Othello's obvious sense of self could let innuendo drive him to his crime? How many other parallels in other literature can you find of the jealous husband (or wife) slowly succumbing to suggestion, resulting in such a tragic end? Are these other works any more plausible? Why or why not?

Lecture Thirty—Transcript
Othello: "The Noble Moor"

A quick way to place Othello in Shakespearean context is to say that he's the opposite of Hamlet. Hamlet is young, he's a university student, he's coming to grips with the world and its realities. Othello is middle-aged, late 30s, early 40s. He's seen the world, including exotic parts of it that most of us have never seen, and he's very familiar with the slings and arrows of outrageous fortune. Hamlet is a student; Othello is a solder. Hamlet is European; Othello is African. Both are princes. Othello mentioned that he fetches his being from men of noble siege, of royal siege. Othello's behavior is not dependent on that inherited rank in the way that Hamlet's is. He has left his original country, whatever that was, and lives among Europeans on the basis of what he has achieved, what he can do, what he has done. It is true, but not very important, that he was born great. It is both true and important that he has achieved greatness, even before the play has started. Perhaps the most important contrast between Hamlet and Othello lies in the matter of their respective freedom.

Hamlet is not free. In no respect did he create the situation in which he finds himself at the start of his play. He was born the prince of a certain country; his father was murdered; his mother married a man he detests; he is not permitted to return to Wittenburg to continue his university career as he would like. He has a duty imposed upon him by a ghost. He greatly resents the situation in which he is placed: "The time is out of joint: O cursed spite / That I was ever born to set it right." He cannot escape that situation. He cannot choose even to die; suicide is forbidden by divine command. The relationship most dependent on human choice, the relationship of love, is a failure for him. Forbidden by Polonius, Ophelia withdraws from Hamlet and returns the love tokens that he has given her, and thus excites his jealous suspicion.

Othello, on the other hand, is very much a self-made man. He's not bound by his past, bound by his circumstances. His past is, in fact, a fascinating exotic narrative, which gives him a certain power over the present; the narrative of his history is what enables him to win the love of Desdemona. His mother has bequeathed him a handkerchief with magic in the web, but she presents no current claim upon him. His position in the Venetian state is contractual. He is a condottiere. He is a soldier of war, a very great distinction, who's been hired by the Senate of Venice to command the Venetian armies. This was a familiar position in Renaissance Italian city-states, the condottiere who runs the troops. These people were held in tremendous respect. In fact, there is a statue in Florence by Donatello of a condottiere called Gattamelata. There is another one in Venice of a condottiere called Colleoni, sculpted by Verocchio—great heroic statues of generals on horseback. This is the kind of distinguished position that Othello holds.

The Venetian Senate are what he calls "my very noble and approved good masters," and to them he owes loyalty. But they are his masters because he and they have chosen that it should be so. Presumably, that relationship could be ended at any time they decided. They need him, in fact, more than he needs them. They need him to protect Venice against the Turks. That is, his loyalties are not the conflicting kind that he inherits, the sort of loyalties that Hamlet has. They are those few loyalties that he has chosen, and for him, the choice of love, above all, has been supremely free. The relation between Othello and Desdemona owes nothing to circumstance, nothing to inherited givens. It successfully defies the surrounding circumstances. Love flourishes between a middle-aged African wanderer and a young Venetian aristocrat because they have chosen that it should, despite their unlikeness and despite whatever anyone else may say about it.

There is claustrophobia that occurs toward the end of this play; I mentioned that in an earlier lecture. But the claustrophobia is all the greater because the acts of freedom are so strong at the beginning—Othello's choice of Desdemona, Desdemona's defense of her choice of Othello in front of the whole Senate, even Iago's choices. Everybody in this play starts by triumphantly asserting their freedom. That's why the end can get so painful, where everybody is so trapped.

Hamlet held a Renaissance ideal of man, that man was "in form and moving how express and admirable, in action how like an angel." Othello does not have the philosophical subtlety of Hamlet; he's not going to quote Pico della Mirandola on the freedom of man. He doesn't need to. He's achieved the Renaissance perfection of action that Hamlet can only dream of. He acts with unfailing resourcefulness in the opening scenes of the play. Until he is enmeshed by jealousy by Iago in the second half of the play, he is in control of whatever contingencies develop. He is courteous, exquisitely courteous to Brabantio when Brabantio is objecting to his marriage to Brabantio's daughter. "Good signior, you shall more command with years / Than with your weapons." Don't put up swords against me, I will respect you as my aged father-in-law. He is very respectful to the Senate, addressing them as "most potent, grave, and reverend signiors, / My very noble and approved good masters." When he has to make a judgment of the drunken Cassio, he marvelously balances his personal affection with the necessary condemnation. Obviously, he has to fire Cassio; you can't have a drunk man in charge of the military garrison in an exposed imperial outpost. At the same time, he doesn't want to repudiate the personal friendship with Cassio, especially since Cassio is now sobering up and obviously feeling just terrible about what he's done in the last hour. Othello says to him, "Cassio, I love thee, / But never more be officer of mine."

His knowledge, as well as his military skill, makes him valuable to the Senate, and they feel able to rely upon him absolutely. Everybody except Iago holds a very high opinion of Othello in this play. Consequently, they find his alteration in the later scenes astonishing. Lodovico arrives from Venice when Othello has fallen into jealous rage and says, "Is this the noble Moor whom our full Senate / Call all in all sufficient?" When Othello has done one of the most painful things he does in public—he slaps his wife Desdemona in front of a crowd of people—Lodovico can only say, "This would not be believed in Venice." I think we have to take that line as an accurate indication of how Othello normally behaves, and what damage Iago has done to him.

The imposing quality of Othello is partly created by verbal elements, by the imposing quality of his speech. Othello talks in a manner unique to himself in what has been described, in a famous essay by Wilson Knight, as "the Othello music." It is a matter of strong verbs, often imperatives, accompanied by brilliantly vivid imagery. That command when the riot breaks out in the first act of the play, one of the first things Othello says in the play, "Keep up your bright swords, for the dew will rust them." It's a matter of picturesque and exotic imagery. He calls the Turks Ottomites; he speaks of the Anthropophagi, "whose heads / Do grow beneath their shoulders."

He talks of the Arabian Sea. He idealizes Desdemona as being one pure chrysolite. Lovely word, chrysolite.

That all-important handkerchief—he describes its origin as "a Sybil ... in her prophetic fury" wove it. It's the sort of thing that might have been made on the Michelangelo ceiling, on the ceiling on the Sistine Chapel; one of those Sybils up there, full of prophetic fury, put it together. Perhaps the most famous speech is the speech when he vows revenge and compares the strength of his vow to the power of the sea rushing through the Hellespont.

> Like to the Pontic Sea,
>
> Whose icy current and compulsive course
>
> Ne'er feels retiring ebb, but keeps due on
>
> To the Propontic and the Hellespont,
>
> Even so my bloody thoughts, with violent pace,
>
> Shall ne'er look back, ne'er ebb to humble love,
>
> Till that a capable and wide revenge
>
> Swallow them up. Now, by yond marble heaven,
>
> In the due reverence of a sacred vow.
>
> I here engage my words.

I can't do it very well. What this needs, the most famous thing it has received in the twentieth century, is the voice of Paul Robeson, who was also a great singer. If you have an opportunity to get a recording of that, or to hear a recording of that, you will find that that great bass voice just rolls across the auditorium like a bass in a Bach oratorio. The language certainly makes it possible. That's a long, careful comparison, the strength of a vow to the power of the sea rushing through the straits. There are grand single words, "Pontic," "Hellespont," "Propontic." Sonorous, aural solids. Of course, the simile involves a physical movement of great majesty, which is reflected in the stateliness of the speech rhythms, in the conceptions, in the formality of the vow, in the utmost, silhouetted clarity of what he is saying.

That is how Othello speaks, and the command, the nobility, the heroic authority of this figure is tremendously reinforced by one more factor: his color. The blackness of Othello is a very complex subject. I cannot handle it adequately in a short lecture; obviously not, because the racial issues are so complicated and so conflicting for us, now, at this time in our history. The issue of the racial difference arouses so many anxieties, distresses and fears. I can say a few things that will stimulate your thought and leave you to work on with the matter.

First, if we think that Othello is deceived by Iago simply because he's black, that is, that Shakespeare thought that black people would be more easily tricked, more easily wrought into murderous passion by a bunch of lies than white people are, then the play is racist, or there is a fundamental racist premise in the play, and I don't want to say any more in defense of it. I don't think that's true, but there are one or two lines which good critics have used to suggest that that assumption sometimes is at work in the play. Second, if we think that Othello believes himself to be inferior to white Europeans, that is, if we think that he has internalized the prejudice of the dominant society amongst which he is now living, then I think we have missed the real self-confidence of the character. I think, in fact, what we've done is to load onto an early seventeenth- century script the history of racism as it has developed in subsequent centuries. Othello is presented as being exotic. He is presented as being distinguished. He is also a welcome guest, frequently invited to Brabantio's household and certainly welcome in the Senate, who eventually applaud his marriage to Desdemona. The only people who express any objection to Othello being Desdemona's husband are Iago, who hates everybody, and Brabantio.

My point is this: Othello has not shared the hideous history of centuries of slavery, of ghetto life, and of subtler forms of discrimination that we now are all too familiar with. He is an African prince at a time when such people were new in European experience. He is different, strikingly different. He is, as we now say, "other." That otherness is not regarded with disdain, except by Iago. The villain of this play is a white man, not a black man. I want to bring up his color in connection with his heroism, with his authority over others, because the blackness is so important on the stage, because the blackness makes him such a striking figure. Even when the issue of his race is not being spoken of, every time he's there on the stage, it is part of our apprehension of him, this magnificent figure. Our eye goes to him every time he appears, in whatever stage grouping.

Shakespeare uses the color in a great many different ways. The Elizabethans certainly did use black also as a term of moral condemnation. When people are angry at Othello late in the play for mistreating Desdemona, then the blackness can be used as a term of moral condemnation. There's a moment when Emilia is very angry, and she says Desdemona "was too fond of her most filthy bargain." There she's using the color in a racially prejudiced way. For most of the time, the color is important for its sheer visual impact. He looks, as well as sounds, separate, free and commanding, utterly his own person. That is why the issue of commitment is so important in this play, that Othello himself speaks of his "unhoused free condition." He has lived a life of freedom; only of certain kinds of contractual arrangements, such as that with the Venetian Senate, which could be ended. The marriage to Desdemona is the one great commitment that changes him, that makes him different. One of his initial responses to the temptation by Iago is to say, "Why did I marry?" It's almost a comic moment; you can imagine anybody saying, in a moment of irritation about the restraints of domestic life, "Why did I do this? I was happier when I was a bachelor, or a spinster, or whatever." His capacity for commitment is all the greater because he starts from that free position.

I've spent all this time stressing the greatness, the heroism of Othello, deliberately, because it seems to me that Shakespearean criticism, criticism of the play, often ignores or belittles the nobility of the Moor. It does so because, late in the play, he does have moments of extraordinary degradation. His jealousy drives him into what looks like an epileptic fit, in which he actually rolls and foams on the floor. Iago sneers at him, standing over his helpless body. Emilia does have that line about "her most filthy bargain." Othello does get subjected to the constant criticism of Iago, and he gets subjected to something else, the constant fault-finding of Shakespearean critics, who find this kind of noble heroic character pompous, self-inflating, or dramatizing. Many Shakespearean critics of the twentieth century have not particularly cared to be taken in, as they consider it to be, taken in by a romantic figure, and I think Othello is a romantic figure.

The chief accusation is that he is stupid. It is the ultimate accusation to be made against anybody in a world of professors and literary critics. He is stupid to be taken in by Iago in the way that he is. Well, okay, he isn't an intellectual like Hamlet. There's no reason he should be; intellectuals don't make good generals. Generals have to act decisively, in emergencies, to take command, which Othello does very well. Hamlet does not. Othello may lack Hamlet's intellectual subtlety, but he is not stupid. He's at least as smart as Macbeth, and nobody has complained about Macbeth being stupid. Both are reasonably smart generals, prompt and heroic. Both get out of their depth because they are being manipulated by people who have a talent for psychic manipulation, who are up to no good. The stupidity charge comes up particularly because we see him accepting a string of lies and insinuations from Iago. That bothers us; we don't want him to believe those things. We forget that we know these characters better than they know each other. We know Iago is a liar; we've heard all his soliloquies. We know he hates Othello; Othello has no idea of that. We know Desdemona is true to him. We forget that Othello doesn't know the others that well; that he naturally trusts in Iago, a fellow soldier with whom he's been through long service; that he doesn't know Desdemona very well; that he doesn't know young Venetian women very well at all. His experience of women is limited.

I do not have the time, and it isn't suitable for the lecture format anyway, to go through the deception of Othello by Iago. It's a very long scene in Act III, Scene III. It's suitable for seminar discussion. You have to talk about line after line, how the various insinuations are planted. But I will take one moment where Iago has corrupted Othello's mind to a certain extent, and Othello makes a key transition, which proves to be fatal. He says, "This fellow's of exceeding honesty / And knows all qualities, with a learned spirit, / Of human dealings." He does trust Iago's experience of human affairs, which is quite extensive; it's just that he's dishonest. He goes on to think about Desdemona:

> If I do prove her haggard,
>
> Though that her jesses were my dear heartstrings,
>
> I'ld whistle her off and let her down the wind
>
> To prey at fortune.

If she is unfaithful to me, if she is likely to stray, if she is haggard, then she's not worth the bother. I'll whistle her off. Then something more happens. That's a possible solution to the problem; if a woman is faithless, forget about her. Then he goes on:

> Haply, for I am black
>
> And have not those soft parts of conversation
>
> That chamberers have,

—I'm not a courtly Venetian—

> or for I am declined
>
> Into the vale of years—yet that's not much—

—I'm middle-aged—

> She's gone. I am abused, and my relief
>
> Must be to loathe her.

"My relief must be to loathe her." That's the key transition, from saying "I'll whistle her off" to saying "My relief / Must be to loathe her;" the movement, not from love to indifference—she's not worth my trouble—but from love to hatred, to rage. It's a move that happens in other Shakespearean plays with white characters. Love, when it leaves, is not replaced by indifference, emptiness. It is replaced by its opposite. If order goes, chaos takes its place. If love goes, hatred, strife, anger takes its place. Othello's mind does begin to collapse. He sees, in fact, his whole world coming apart:

> Farewell the tranquil mind! Farewell content!
>
> Farewell the plumed troop, and the big wars
>
> That make ambition virtue! O, farewell,
>
> Farewell the neighing steed, and the shrill trump,
>
> The spirit-stirring drum, the ear-piercing fife,
>
> The royal banner, and all quality,
>
> Pride, pomp, and circumstance of glorious war! …
>
> Othello's occupation's gone!

His identity was so invested in the relationship with Desdemona that it's altogether gone. His occupation's gone, his generalship, his soldiership. Note that he had considered war to be an order-making activity. That's unusual for us, because we think of war as almost unrelievedly bad. But war, from his point of view, is one of the ways of having order in life, protecting civilization against the outer forces of barbarism, who, in this play, are the Turks. With love going, order goes, his occupation goes, he goes. As a result, we have a succession of horrible scenes: the scene where he demands the handkerchief from Desdemona, which she's accidentally lost, and Iago manages to twist into some kind of flimsy evidence for her infidelity; the scene where he strikes Desdemona in front of Lodovico; the scene in which he treats Desdemona as if she were a worker in a brothel, and Emilia as if she were the madam.

Then he pulls himself together, to some extent, for the last scene. He wants to take revenge on his wife, but he doesn't want it to be an angry revenge. He wants it to be an execution of justice. He comes as a minister of justice, and yet he is crushingly aware of what she means to him. He still loves her. He finally does murder her in rage, but only because she is resisting. It isn't until the last scene of the play that Desdemona understands what's wrong with Othello, what she's been accused of, that she has been accused of adultery with Cassio. "Well, send for Cassio and ask him. It isn't true." The denial enrages Othello, so he kills her in rage, then there follows a curious silence, a curious laconic quality in Othello, as the various discoveries are made.

Emilia realizes what has been happening, that Iago has been telling lies. She's willing to unfold the whole truth. All of it comes out; Cassio comes in and says, "I never gave you cause" and all that kind of thing. During all that stuff, Othello is going through some strange world, where he has lost himself utterly—the original self that was destroyed by the belief in his wife's infidelity, and the second self that was gaining revenge. Somebody comes in and asks, "Where's Othello?" and Othello says, "That's he that was Othello. Here I am"—an utter displacement of himself. He pulls himself together at the last moment to commit suicide. He anticipates the inevitable death penalty that will be passed upon him by a Venetian court, and carries it out himself, with this speech:

> Soft you. a word or two before you go.

I have done the state some service, and they know't.
No more of that...
Speak of me as I am; nothing extenuate,
Nor set down aught in malice. Then must you speak
Of one that loved not wisely but too well;
Of one not easily jealous, but, being wrought,
Perplex'd in the extreme...
Set you down this;
And say besides, that in Aleppo once,
Where a malignant and a turban'd Turk
Beat a Venetian and traduced the state,
I took by the throat the circumcised dog
And smote him, thus.

Cutting his throat on the last line, to the surprise of the others. Why should he remember the incident of the malignant and turbaned Turk who traduced the state? Because he traduced the state. Othello is the defender of Venetian civilization against barbarism, which in this play is represented by the Turks, the malignant and turbaned Turks. This is how he has lived his life; this is how he dies. Only now, the barbarism is in himself. He is the offender who has traduced the state by killing Desdemona. He remains at the end as he was at the beginning—the protector of civilization, the stalwart guardian at the gate.

Lecture Thirty-One
King Lear: "This Is the Worst"

Scope:

King Lear is a towering work, a tragedy in any sense of the word, a moving—even brutal—experience to read or to watch. It is a complex play, with double plots, intrigue, psychological depth, physical and emotional horror. It is a play of disintegration, of coming apart, socially, psychologically, emotionally, physically. In this first of three lectures, we will focus on this theme of disintegration.

Outline

I. *King Lear* has proved to be the most painful of Shakespeare's tragedies for our time. *Hamlet* was considered to be the greatest of the tragedies in the 19th century; Lear is considered to be the greatest in the 20th century.

  A. It is painful in term of physical atrocities: blinding, madness, exposure of old men to storms, murders.

  B. It is emotionally painful in terms of verbal and emotional exchanges: bargaining for love, cursing people to sterility, rebuking helpless people, feelings of shame.

II. The chief dramatic techniques by which the play brings people from positions of power and prosperity to the condition of "poor, bare, forked animals" are repetition and disintegration.

  A. In contrast to the variety of *Hamlet*, everything that happens in the opening scenes of *King Lear* happens several times: banishments, abuse of fathers, multiple mad scenes. There is a full double plot. The language is full of repetition.

  B. An ordered kingdom, with an enthroned king commanding obedience from his hierarchically ordered subjects and family, is reduced to a collection of poorly clad or naked people in a storm speaking random dialogue.

III. The disintegration is most vividly shown on a personal level in Edgar's soliloquy "I have heard myself proclaimed" (2.3).

  A. He has lost his social position and his inheritance, and is pursued as a criminal. He adopts nakedness, mutilation, and madness as a disguise.

B. There are numerous thematic elements here:
1. Loss of civilized trappings
2. Reduction of a character to a bestial level
3. Madness, forcing unwilling and scarcely clad humans to give alms to their fellows
4. Identity (e.g., Edgar has been disowned by his father, Gloucester. As Tom o'Bedlam, he is no longer Edgar).

IV. The implications of this disintegration are most vividly shown on social and cosmic levels in Lear's speech "O most small fault" (1.4.265–271), which reflects an Elizabethan conception of the universe. This speech can be compared with Othello's speech in the last lecture.

A. The Elizabethans thought of the universe is a battleground between strife, which produces chaos, and love, which creates and sustains orderly nature.
1. Once love is withdrawn, life and the universe move toward chaos.
2. The storms are good symbols of strife entering the world.

B. In the first three acts of *King Lear*, the withdrawal of love produces personal, social, and cosmic chaos. Both Lear and Edgar go through the same transitions.

Essential Reading:

Shakespeare, *King Lear*.

Supplementary Reading/Viewing:

See videotape of *King Lear* (the one directed by Michael Elliott and starring Laurence Olivier is better than the BBC version).

Goldman, *Shakespeare and the Energies of Drama*, chapter 7.

Questions to Consider:

1. Consider the use of repetition in *King Lear*. Is so much of it necessary? What would be the effect without the double plots, mad scenes, or other thematically echoing scenes?

2. Compare Lear to Othello in terms of psychological disintegration, specifically, in their attempts to control a crumbling universe (whether personal or public).

Lecture Thirty-One—Transcript
King Lear: "This Is the Worst"

To this first lecture on *King Lear*, I have given the subtitle "This Is the Worst." That is a line from the fourth act of the play, said by Edgar, and raising the question whether we can ever say of a situation, "This is the worst that can happen." As a matter of fact, although things are very bad for Edgar at that moment, what happens next is he finds out that his father has been horribly blinded. He concludes, we can never say this is the worst. Something dreadful may always happen yet. That is characteristic of the play of *King Lear*, and one of the reasons why the play of *King Lear* has been considered so important in the twentieth century. Hamlet was the dominating tragedy of Shakespeare's tragedies for the nineteenth century. The nineteenth century found in Hamlet's doubts, delays, and intellectual puzzlement a reflection of their own intellectual condition. The wars, genocides, and other atrocities of the twentieth century have made *King Lear* speak more deeply to many people. This is probably the most painful of Shakespeare's tragedies for our time.

The pain is physical. There are mad scenes. There is a scene with three madmen in it simultaneously. There is nakedness; people are sent out with very little clothing into a terrible storm. There are murders onstage. There is perhaps the worst atrocity in all Shakespeare; a helpless old man is blinded on the stage. It can be a shocking moment. Even if you know the script and know that that's going to happen, it can be staged in a way that shocks you deeply. There are physical things that are very painful. There are emotional things that can be equally painful, if it is possible to compare emotional pain with physical pain; I'm not sure.

In the first scene, King Lear is bargaining for love, asking his daughters, "Tell me how much you love me. I'll give you thus much land if you say you love me enough." We all want to be loved, and I'm afraid we all want others to tell us they love us. I've heard one critic say, "'Tell me how much you love me' is a thing that we say implicitly or explicitly, and are so ashamed of it that we don't even mention to our therapist that we have said it." Nonetheless, it is mortifying to watch Lear do that, put himself through that process. Other emotional pain; there is cursing. Lear curses Goneril to sterility. They're very angry at each other; she's as angry at him as he is at her at that time. Nonetheless, whatever she may be, it is hard for any woman to stand there with her father saying directly to her, "May the gods convey sterility into your womb." There is painful rebuking. Even before Gloucester is blinded, when he's tied to a chair, Regan and Cornwall humiliate him. Regan plucks him by the beard, a very great insult to his masculinity, to his humanity. Even more subtlely, there are moments of pain in scenes that are by and large tender. The scene where Lear emerges from madness and finds himself within the tender care of his loving daughter Cordelia. He cannot really believe that she does love him. He has treated her badly, and that's all he can think of, so he is humiliated and says things like, "I pray you, do not mock me. Do not laugh at me. I know you do not love me." For an old man to say that to his daughter— well, as I say, it is emotionally very painful.

A great deal happens in this play, and I must, in this case as in other cases, cut through much material that I could talk about. I will try to summarize what goes on by stressing the major dramatic techniques that Shakespeare uses. At the start of his play, King Lear is the most powerful and successful king in Shakespeare. He has ruled for many years. Britain is at peace and entirely obedient; neighboring kings kneel at his throne, begging for the hand of his youngest daughter. Powerful dukes have married his two elder daughters, while leaving the size of the dowry entirely up to Lear's will. This is not a matter that's been bargained over as part of the betrothal processes. It's entirely in Lear's hand, and he's about to divide up the kingdom in whatever way suits his fancy. No other ruler in Shakespeare—not Henry V after Agincourt, or Octavius Caesar after the death of Marc Antony—has the whole thing packaged up so completely. Then it all goes to pieces.

The principal techniques by which Shakespeare has it go to pieces in the first half of the play are repetition and disintegration. First, repetition. In *Hamlet*, as I mentioned in a previous lecture, the action is marked by variety. There are always new stimuli. There are courtiers and guards. There are ghosts and there are gravediggers. There are students and soldiers, princes, players, and pirates. In *Lear*, everything is repeated. Lear banishes Cordelia, and then in the same scene he banishes Kent. He is abused by Goneril near the end of Act I; near the end of Act II, he is abused by Regan. When the mad king and his mad jester go out into the storm, they encounter there a mad beggar. After two mad scenes, Lear disappears for 500 lines, then he returns for a third mad scene. The whole thing happens all over again in the subplot about the Gloucester family; similar misjudgments, similar abuse of a helpless father. This is the only one of Shakespeare's major tragedies with a fully developed subplot running beside the main plot from beginning to end, so that everything has to happen at least twice. The subplot contains the blinding, and Shakespeare stages that so even that is a repetition. You'd think the blinding would be just one action, but no. Cornwall plucks out one eye of Gloucester, and then he's interrupted. One of his own servants stands up against him, saying, "I never did you better service than to stop you from doing this terrible thing," and he attacks Cornwall. This servant is eventually killed, but it takes a little time, so we go back, after some minutes, to pluck out the other eye of Gloucester.

Even the language reflects this relentless repetition. At the beginning of the play, Lear asks Cordelia, "What can you say to draw / A third more opulent than your sisters? Speak." Cordelia answers, "Nothing, my lord." "Nothing?" "Nothing." "Nothing will come of nothing. Speak again." At the end of the play, over her corpse, Lear says, "She'll come no more. / Never, never, never, never, never." One word said five times. If you think that Shakespeare always writes fancy language, you're wrong. He gets tremendous effects by writing very simply indeed.

The other major technique for the first half of *King Lear* is disintegration. The opening scene presents us with a visual image of an ordered kingdom. Lear is on his throne, everybody else responds to his commands. Rank and position are indicated by appropriate clothing, by crowns, by coronets. Relationships are manifest in feudal titles—king, duke, earl, servant—and in family roles—daughter, husband. The action is rational, the formal transfer of power from one generation to the next. Even the dialogue reflects this firm structure; with only a trivial exception or two, Lear speaks every other speech. Everything, in other words, is either said by Lear or to him. Everyone else is defined by his or her response to Lear's demands for love and obedience.

By the middle of the play, by the middle of Act III, all of this has disintegrated. At the heart of the play, there is a scene in which Kent, who is disguised, and Gloucester bring Lear, the fool, and Edgar, who is also disguised, to a hovel for shelter in the middle of a storm.

Two of the characters, as I say, are in disguise. Kent is an earl; he is now a nameless servant. Edgar, who is the son of an earl, the heir of an earl, is now calling himself Tom o'Bedlam. That not only erases their ranks, but also Edgar's family relationship to Gloucester, who does not recognize his own son. Two of the characters are genuinely mad, Lear and the fool. Edgar is feigning madness so well that we may wonder if the pretense isn't passing over into the reality. Edgar is naked, or perhaps just has a cloth around his middle. Lear, in the previous scene, had tried to tear off at least some of his clothing. The action of this scene in the middle is chaotic. Lear tries to conduct a trial of his ungrateful daughters, with himself as prosecutor, with Kent the disguised servant, Edgar the disguised madman, and the fool as the judges, and two warped wooden stools standing in for the defendants. That is the reduction, the disintegration of the opening royal picture of Lear on his throne, handing down his judgments in an orderly fashion. In this case, the dialogue is random; the words of legal process are interspersed with hallucinatory ravings, dirty jokes, and old songs.

I've been generalizing about the first two and one-half acts. Let me spend a little time talking about one particular scene, one particular speech, which happens to be a whole scene, to pin this process down. This is Act II, Scene III, the speech of Edgar, when he decides to go into disguise. Edgar is the eldest son of Gloucester, and Gloucester, his father, has been made to believe that Edgar is plotting against him. Therefore, Edgar has to go into hiding, with Gloucester's soldiers after him, pursuing him on a charge of attempted murder. Edgar says in soliloquy to us:

> I have heard myself proclaim'd,
> And by the happy hollow of a tree
> Escap'd the hunt. No port is free, no place
> That guard, and most unusual vigilance,
> Does not attend my taking. Whiles I may 'scape,
> I will preserve myself; and am bethought
> To take the basest and most poorest shape
> That ever penury, in contempt of man,
> Brought near to beast. My face I'll grime with filth,
> Blanket my loins, elf all my hairs in knots,

And with presented nakedness outface

The winds and persecutions of the sky.

The country gives me proof and precedent

Of Bedlam beggars, who, with roaring voices,

Strike in their numb'd and mortified bare arms

Pins, wooden pricks, sprigs, nails of rosemary;

And with this horrible object, from low farms,

Poor pelting villages, sheepcotes, and mills,

Sometime with lunatic bans, sometime with prayers,

Enforce their charity. 'Poor Turlygod! poor Tom!'

That's something yet! Edgar I nothing am.

Let me talk about that speech. In the first place, it is exposition, absolutely necessary exposition. It tells us what Edgar is going to do. We need the preparation. The next time we see him, he's going to pop out of a hovel in the middle of the storm and encounter Lear and the fool, and the sudden apparition of this weird creature, Tom o'Bedlam, will drive Lear mad. We'd better be in a position to identify who that creature is, so the speech sets that up.

More significantly, a whole series of thematic statements are being made here. Edgar says he is going to strip himself, go forth with presented nakedness. That makes literal, actual, visible on the stage, something that has only been metaphorical in the language hitherto. Lear, in the very first scene of the play, said he would divest himself of rule, a demand taking off certain clothes. Edgar literalizes that. He will be stripped altogether of civilized trappings. It is not only a stripping, it is a bestialization. He is going to be man brought near to beast. In the middle of the play, men are brought down to the level of animals. Lear, Edgar, Kent, and the fool go through the storm as if they were animals without proper shelter, unhoused. Gloucester, in the blinding scene, thinks of himself as being tied to the stake and obliged to stand the course. The metaphor is taken from the savage Elizabethan sport of bear-baiting, where the bear was chained by the neck to a stake, and savage hungry dogs were set on to attack him. He couldn't run away, therefore he had to fight back. The wicked characters become animals too. Albany calls his wife and her sister monsters of the deep, sharks.

Nakedness; bestiality; the third theme in this speech of Edgar's is, of course, madness. Edgar will play the role of a Bedlam beggar; that is, a man who has been in Bethlehem Hospital. The full name of the hospital was The Hospital of St. Mary of Bethlehem, and it was founded somewhere in the thirteenth century, so it's terribly anachronistic for this play of *King Lear* which is happening in pre-Christian times, but never mind; Shakespeare's full of anachronisms. Don't let them bother you, or if you do let them bother you, you'll never get through Shakespeare. The name "Hospital of St. Mary of Bethlehem" was gradually worn down, smoothed down to be just Bedlam, which is the origin of our word "bedlam," meaning a scene of chaos and disorder. What the Elizabethans did in Shakespeare's time—the state did not want to care for any more mad folk than they had to. They put the dangerous ones in Bedlam, but if someone was a relatively calm and unhurtful madman, they would let him go out, go around earning his income by helping people, whatever chores that a madman might do. The generic name for these people was Tom, Tom from Bedlam, Tom o'Bedlam. They would live on people's charity. Edgar stresses that; the object of this bedlam beggary is, as he says, to enforce charity, "sometime with lunatic bans, sometime with prayers." The prayers are, of course, normal begging; lunatic bans would be cursing. You curse people in hopes of forcing them to give you money.

Edgar's object is, in other words, to make unwilling human beings give to their fellow men. He really does mean "to enforce." Consider the way he will look. To sum up the picture I'm describing: grimy; nearly naked; his hair in a tangle, "elf-locks;" he will have a roaring voice; his arms will bear the marks of horrible self-mutilation. When he actually gets to playing Tom o'Bedlam, the character he invents turns out to have a masochistic obsession with sin and punishment. "The devils are at me for my sins," and he keeps beating himself. Poor Tom is perfectly awful. It is easy to overlook that when you are only reading the play.

Sometimes, onstage, actors don't follow through thoroughly. After all, it's the young male lead part of the play, the longest part for a young man. So, in a company, the part is usually played by your leading romantic hero, who will turn up next week playing Bassanio, Sebastian, Laertes or someone like that. If you strip him naked, the guy looks kind of attractive. The point is not that; he is supposed to look utterly hideous. He is not the kind of sweet beggar whom you give money to out of a warm feeling of human solidarity. He's the kind of beggar who shoves his stump in your face. You give him money, not out of a warm feeling of human charity, but because you want him to go away. You can't bear that, and he may be yelling at you with a roaring voice, lunatic bans.

The final theme I am concerned with in this speech is the theme of identity, the last lines of the soliloquy. "Poor Turlygod, poor Tom. / That's something yet. Edgar I nothing am." As Lear has been in the opening acts reduced to nothing, giving away his crown, giving away his power, losing his knights, so also the role of Edgar has been reduced to nothing, that key word in these opening scenes. In a feudal society, of course, the identity of a young man depends heavily on being his father's son. Edgar was born to be heir of Gloucester; everything in his life is determined by being the eldest son of an earl. Gloucester has disowned him; everything is gone. He is reduced to nothing. As Poor Tom, this identity that he invents, he may be something; something may come out of that. Nothing will come of nothing. This is an extremely useful speech with which to anchor the important issues of the play, the process that takes place in the first two and one-half acts.

Edgar, of course, is in the subplot. For the last section of this lecture, I had better move back to the main plot; for Lear also has a speech that provides terms for grasping the disintegration that happens in the first half of the play. Under pressure from the rudeness of Goneril, the jibes of the fool, the misbehavior of Oswald, Lear begins to think, in the long scene at the end of Act I, that he had overreacted to Cordelia saying "Nothing" in response to his demand for love, to Cordelia's apparent disobedience. In the middle of that quarrel with Goneril in Act I, Scene IV, Lear suddenly says, as a kind of aside that Goneril doesn't hear, that really is meant for the audience:

> O most small fault,
>
> How ugly didst thou in Cordelia show!
>
> Which, like an engine, wrench'd my frame of nature
>
> From the fix'd place; drew from my heart all love
>
> And added to the gall. O Lear, Lear, Lear!
>
> Beat at this gate that let thy folly in
>
> And thy dear judgment out!

I want to talk about that speech. Lear has a "frame of nature," which he believes is normally fixed, but was wrenched awry by Cordelia's fault. Consequently, he lost all love. He still thinks there was some fault in Cordelia; it's only in the next scene where he flatly says, " I did her wrong" and assumes all the blame himself. It's now only a small fault, but he overreacted to it. He is saying that. He's going through a process very much like what happened to Othello in the speech I isolated in the previous lecture, when he said, "If I do prove her haggard, I'll whistle her off, forget about her," and then five lines later, is saying, "My relief must be to loathe her." Lear, like Othello, goes from love to absolute hatred. He cannot pause in the middle state of indifference, of not caring. When love disappears, it is replaced by hatred, strife, a desire for revenge.

As a matter of fact, these words connect the action of the play to a whole Elizabethan conception of the universe, that I could have explained when I was talking about *Othello* and I had better explain in more detail now. One conception of the Elizabethan universe I have already used previously in these lectures, that is, the hierarchical conception, that God created everything in a vertical order. At the top are angels, who come in nine ranks. Below that are human beings, and men are higher than women, kings are higher than peasants, and so forth. Below that are animals, below that are plants, below that are elements. In each, there are subhierarchies within the big hierarchies, so that the lion is the king of beasts, and the diamond is the greatest of stones, the cedar is the greatest of trees, and so forth.

That is the most familiar Elizabethan world picture, the one that Tillyard wrote his book about, but there is another, more dynamic conception of the Elizabethan universe that is, in fact, more helpful to Shakespeare in writing plays because it is dynamic. It comes up over and over again, especially in the tragedies. In this view, the initial state of the material universe was chaos, everything in disorder, the hot, the cold, the wet and the dry—every atom in constant strife with every other atom, nothing shaped into any forms. When God created the world, God's spirit moved over this chaos. The spirit of God is, of course, love, and love took part of that chaos and colonized it, shaped the atoms into stable forms. From that, we get the forms and usual motions of the universe; the stars, the planets, the sun and the earth move in certain patterns, and atoms cohere together to make animals, plants, men and so forth.

As long as love prevails, that universe is sustained. Love is necessary for an orderly condition of nature. Once love is withdrawn, then nature begins to revert toward the original condition of chaos. That is, we have two opposed conditions—chaos, total lack of form; and nature, everything proper, orderly form. Elemental strife is what prevails in chaos, and love is what prevails in nature. When love is withdrawn, then the strife begins to invade. It's what happens in all the Shakespearean tragedies; because there is some loss of love, then strife begins to take over the human universe. It's why there are always storms, or nearly always storms, in Shakespearean tragedy; the storm is so good a symbol of strife coming back into the world. There are storms in *Lear*, in *Macbeth*, in *Julius Caesar*.

Let me apply that to what is going on here in the play itself. For Lear himself, he began as a king in charge of everything, trying to behave in a rational fashion. He was moved into wrath; that's the invasion of strife. He ends up in a state of total psychic chaos, which is madness, chaos in the head. Likewise Edgar—he begins as the heir to an earldom; he is then dispossessed of that position, thrown out of the order. He goes into madness too, although in his case, it's a pretended madness adopted as a disguise to protect himself.

It happens to the society as well. That stable, orderly society that we saw in the first scene, with the king on his throne, handing down his rulings and everybody obeying him, moves into a condition of family strife, with daughters disobeying their fathers, with daughters throwing their fathers out into the storm, and then worse and worse; plots of murder, mutilation, the blinding of Gloucester, and ultimately war. On a social level as well, there is chaos. Behind it all is the natural backdrop, nature herself, the outer world of rocks, trees, stones, air, and fire. That goes into chaos, the chaos of the great storm that occupies the middle of the play and calls for more storm directions than occur in any other Shakespeare play. Kent says of it, "There has never been a storm like this. I have lived on this earth for 48 [sic 88] years, four score and eight years on my back, and I've never seen a storm like this. This is the elemental storm, total chaos." That is the pattern of the opening of *King Lear*.

Lecture Thirty-Two
King Lear: Wisdom Through Suffering

Scope:

The title of this lecture derives from the *Agamemnon* of Aeschylus. There is immense suffering in both plays and from this comes wisdom for the characters (and for the spectators as well). As the theme of Lecture 31 was "disintegration," the theme of this lecture is "coping," particularly coping that leads to personal insight and growth on the part of the characters.

Outline

I. Since atrocities recur in *King Lear*, a frequent action of the play is coping, that is, people's effort to deal emotionally and intellectually with disaster.

   A. Gloucester's response to the supposed schemes of Edgar in Act 1 Scene 2 offers a typical example of coping techniques: rage, denial, and attempted explanation. Lear has the same reactions to Cordelia in the first scene.

   B. Act 4 offers "malice of the gods" as a reason for the suffering.
      1. This coping mechanism relies on an astrological explanation.
      2. Edmund demolishes this weak argument and places responsibility on human nature itself.
      3. Gloucester then advances another possible explanation: the gods who kill men for sport.

   C. In Act 5, Edgar offers an explanation—justice of the gods is being visited on the sufferers because of Gloucester's adultery that resulted in the birth of Edmund.

II. Gloucester moves through various further stages of response as the plot unfolds.

   A. In Act 2, as Lear's relationship with his daughters deteriorates, he tries to compromise, to "have all well betwixt you."

B. In Act 3, he tries secret action and defiance. He shows himself to be on Lear's side against his (Lear's) wicked daughters. He takes his actions secretly, but is betrayed by Edmund and is blinded.

C. In Act 4, he collapses and seeks to die.

III. Edgar's movement is one of growth.

    A. He experiences complete abasement as Tom o'Bedlam.

    B. He kills the two men who curiously mirror his own condition, his half-brother Edmund and the steward Oswald. He thus becomes those things against which he later fights.

    C. He emerges as a heroic knight and presumably the next king of Britain in the final act. His progress appears to be a surrealistic version of the education of Prince Hal in the *Henry IV* plays.

IV. Lear manifests a remarkable capacity for taking in new experience.

    A. He recognizes his own responsibility for mistreating Cordelia by the end of Act 1.

    B. Amid his anger and cursing in Act 2, he also recognizes the need for patience and the need to grow morally.

    C. He comes to empathize with a kind of suffering he had not known about before: he prays for the "poor naked wretches" (3.4.28–36) in a plea for distributive justice.

    D. He finds a fundamental embodiment of the human condition in mad Tom o'Bedlam.

Essential Reading:

Shakespeare, *King Lear*.

Supplementary Reading:

Danby, *Shakespeare's Doctrine of Nature*.

Halio, Introduction to *King Lear* (New Cambridge edition).

Howard, *Shakespeare's Art of Orchestration* (references to *King Lear*).

Questions to Consider:

1. Are there other coping mechanisms in this play that were not discussed in the lecture? Identify them and give examples (Act and Scene) where they occur.

2. Compare the growth of Edgar with that of Prince Hal. What are the similarities and differences in their "apprenticeship" for kingship?

The subtitle of this second lecture on *King Lear* is "Wisdom through Suffering." I take the phrase from Aeschylus, where it occurs in the *Agamemnon*, the first chorus, "Wisdom comes only through suffering." It is perhaps too optimistic a phrase to use. I am not sure that wisdom in fact comes through suffering; only of the assurance that it will only come through suffering if it comes at all. There are atrocities in *King Lear*. Since they frequently occur, a frequent action on the part of the characters of the play is trying to cope with those atrocities, people's effort to deal emotionally and intellectually with disaster, to account for it.

I want to start by taking some examples from the part of Gloucester, the central figure of the subplot. What happens to his mind as he tries to cope with the events of *King Lear*? In the second scene of the play, he's trying to cope with a very unpalatable fact: the revelation of the supposed villainy of his legitimate heir, Edgar. Edmund has convinced him that Edgar is plotting against his life. He responds to that by saying:

> O villain, villain! His very opinion in the letter! Abhorred villain! Unnatural, detested, brutish villain! worse than brutish! Go, sirrah, seek him; I'll apprehend him. Abominable villain! Where is he?

His initial response is the gut response, sheer rage. We can be very angry when we are told unpleasant truths. That response does not last; it soon becomes a different one. The second response is incredulity, disbelief: "He cannot be such a monster." That's not quite disbelief, that's what we now call denial, the desire not to believe—I refuse to believe it. Lear has the same reactions to Cordelia back in the first scene. It's a little simpler here; less time is devoted to it. That's why I'm using Gloucester as an example; it's easier to make a point. But these two actions on Lear's and Gloucester's part are analogous. *King Lear* is about two deluded old gentlemen; it is an aspect of the relentless repetitiousness of the play.

I have, however, referred to what Gloucester discovers here as a truth. The delusion is only superficial. They make, both Lear and Gloucester, drastic mistakes about which of their children to trust, but they are both in the process of discovering a very unpleasant truth, namely that some children do hate their parents. The play is built on that truth. *King Lear* is, in part, about the reaction to the discovery. The reaction in Gloucester's case is first anger, and then the desire not to believe. He doesn't stop there. There's a third response, a movement from emotional reaction to mental reaction. Merely feeling about it isn't enough; he tries to find an explanation for the supposed villainy of Edgar:

> These late eclipses in the sun and moon portend no good to us. Though the wisdom of nature can reason it thus and thus, yet nature finds itself scourged with the sequent effects. Love cools, friendship falls off, brothers divide. In cities, mutinies; in countries, discord; in palaces, treason; and the bond cracked 'twixt son and father. This villain of mine comes under the prediction; there's son against father: the king falls from the bias of nature; there's father against child. We have seen the best of our time. Machinations, hollowness, treachery, all ruinous disorders, follow us disquietly to our graves.

The answer, the explanation offered is supernatural; supernatural forces are responsible for the villainy of Edgar. Man's destiny is controlled by the late eclipses of the sun and moon. The stars hold our destiny. I am inclined to think, as explanations go, this is a pretty poor one. Astrology may be a parlor game for some of you, but Shakespeare doesn't show any tendency to believe in it. Occasionally, he will use events in the heavens to symbolize or correspond to events on the earth. There are comets the night before Julius Caesar dies, but they don't cause the assassination of Julius Caesar. We see Brutus and Cassius plotting that assassination.

Indeed, in the case of Gloucester, we're immediately encouraged to feel how poor his explanation is by Edmund. As soon as Gloucester has left the stage, his bastard son explodes the whole idea:

> This is the excellent foppery of the world, that, when we are sick in fortune—often the surfeit of our own behaviour—we make guilty of our disasters the sun, moon, and stars; as if we were villains on heavenly compulsion; fools by necessity; knaves, thieves, and treachers … by a divine thrusting on. An admirable evasion of whore-master man, to lay his goatish disposition to the charge of a star! My father compounded with my mother under the dragon's tail, and

my nativity was under Ursa Major, so that it follows, I am rough and lecherous. Tut! I should have been that I am, had the maidenliest star in the firmament twinkled on my bastardizing."

In other words, Edmund is saying that Gloucester is evading, evading "whore-master man." Specifically, he's evading two things; evading the fact that people are vile, that very often, we do very bad things. Gloucester goes through the first half of the play trying to deny what's going on. He's also evading, according to Edmund, the fact that we are responsible for this vileness. When we are sick in our fortunes, it is often because of the surfeit of our own nature. If we blame the stars, the gods, or what have you, we are shortcutting responsibility. As I've suggested, I think we feel Gloucester's evasion to be evasive without much prodding. We're not likely to adopt the kind of explanation he offers here. But the habit of mind that he reveals is characteristic in this play. People in *King Lear* continually try to evade man's whore-master-like nature by means of large philosophical explanations.

It is Gloucester again who enunciates the most famous of these. In Act IV, when he's been through a terrible experience, the physical agony of blinding, the revelation to himself that Edgar, his good son, was good, and therefore that he has mistreated Edgar, so he concludes, "As flies to wanton boys are we to the gods. / They kill us for their sport." We are like flies, or butterflies, in the hands of silly little boys, wanton boys. Did you ever, when you were a child, tear the wings off a butterfly to see what it would do? No? Perhaps you cut the tails off a salamander instead, playing little experiments on helpless animals. Gloucester's statement is a great one, powerful and resonant, a great line. "As flies to wanton boys are we to the gods. / They kill us for their sport." Often it has been taken as the meaning of *King Lear*, but it too may be an evasion. It may be a necessary evasion; at this particular moment, that statement probably helps Gloucester to preserve his sanity. It does contain at least a hypothetical truth; if there are gods in the universe of *King Lear*, they must be capable of terrible malevolence toward men. But it is an evasion nonetheless, for even if there are gods, they do not need to tear off the wings of men and women. Regan and Cornwall can do that very nicely for themselves, without any divine assistance. In doing so, they do get assistance, not from the gods, but from silly old men like Gloucester, who are so ignorant that they do not know their own children, that they trust the treacherous one and expel the faithful one.

King Lear, as a play, insists on the vileness of human beings. The gods get blamed only secondarily, if they come in at all. All the good characters in the play are aware of gods; they frequently speak about the gods, speculate about what sorts of gods there could be in this world. But what is actually said of them varies enormously; multiple views are expressed. Many of them contain the kind of partial or hypothetical truth I just mentioned. No single view seems to contain the whole truth. In the last scene if the play, Edgar has a statement that is diametrically opposed to Gloucester's statement about the flies. He says of his father's own career:

> The gods are just, and of our pleasant vices
>
> Make instruments to scourge us.
>
> The dark and vicious place where thee he got
>
> Cost him his eyes.

He's talking to Edmund. Edmund is a bastard; Gloucester's adultery with an unnamed woman led to the conception of Edmund and, therefore, eventually to the blinding of his father. The ultimate just result, according to Edgar, of Gloucester's sexual failing is his blinding. Is that an evasion? At least the causal sequence is right; the adultery was one of the deeds that led to the blinding. Edmund did betray his father to Cornwall and Regan, and they did the blinding. The dark deed contributes to the dark result. But the notion of justice is very odd indeed. Because of one act of adultery, you deserve to have your eyes gouged out? That seems very severe to me.

Even if you do accept it as an act of justice, what about Cordelia? A few minutes after those lines of Edgar's that I've just quoted, Albany says of Cordelia, "The gods defend her." The next thing that happens is, enter Lear with Cordelia dead in his arms. The gods don't seem to do much defending of good people. We want the idea of justice; we dignify events with it. An unjust world is frighteningly unsafe. The idea of divine justice stands in the way of, removes the possibility of, that terrifying notion that the gods are malicious boys sporting with us. But Edgar's aphorism about the justice of the gods seems to me as incomplete as any other generalization in the play.

I've jumped forward to talk about these generalizations about the gods and left Gloucester himself behind. Gloucester, in fact, moves through various stages of response as the plot unfolds. In Act II, as Lear's relationship with his daughters deteriorates, Gloucester tries to compromise, tries to "make all well betwixt you," and, in doing so, continues denying how severe the disagreements are. In Act III, however, his fundamental loyalties come out. He is basically on Lear's side; Lear is his old master, has been his king. He does indeed attempt to save Lear from the wickedness of his daughters, tries to shelter Lear in the storm, hears of a plot against Lear's life, and gets him away secretly to Dover. All that is done behind the backs of Regan, Cornwall, and Goneril. It is all secret action, which he hopes will remain secret. He is betrayed by Edmund to Regan and Cornwall, and brought in as a captive to face their version of justice.

There we get some measure of the man's strength. He does pluck up enough strength to be defiant against Regan and Cornwall. "I am tied to the stake, and I must stand the course." Regan asks, "Wherefore did you send him to Dover?"

> Because I would not see thy cruel nails
>
> Pluck out his poor old eyes; nor thy fierce sister
>
> In his anointed flesh stick boarish fangs.
>
> The sea, with such a storm as his bare head
>
> In hell-black night endur'd, would have buoy'd up
>
> And quench'd the stellared stars.
>
> Yet, poor old heart, he holp the heavens to rain. …
>
> I shall see
>
> The winged vengeance overtake such children.

That's an extremely courageous statement for him to make; he's tied to a chair against these people, whom he now knows to be capable of considerable violence, and he pays for it instantly. Cornwall says, "See't shalt thou never.... / Upon these eyes of thine I'll set my foot," and he proceeds with the blinding. That is a further terrible blow for Gloucester. In Act IV, he has seen enough. The revelation of human ghastliness in Regan and Cornwall, the knowledge of his own contribution to the abuse of Edgar, all of these things move him toward despair. He feels he cannot go further. He says to poor Tom o'Bedlam, who is, of course, his son, but he doesn't know that:

> There is a cliff, whose high and bending head
> Looks fearfully in the confined deep.
> Bring me but to the very brim of it,
> And I'll repair the misery thou dost bear
> With something rich about me. From that place
> I shall no leading need.

He's going to commit suicide. Life is unbearable, with his own guilt and with the horrible behavior of other people. That is Gloucester's movement. His son Edgar has a different kind if movement. I've already touched on this by dealing with his disguise soliloquy in the previous lecture. Now I'll move on to the mad scenes in the middle of the play, where something astonishing happens, something that, in fact, is not realistic at all; but then, as I've said before, Shakespeare doesn't write realistic plays. It is surrealistic drama we get with Edgar's disguise as Tom o'Bedlam. This young man, who had been a complete dupe, totally manipulated by his brother in Acts I and II, has turned into a master playwright and actor, creating and sustaining the role of Tom o'Bedlam, the professional madman, with such remarkable virtuosity that Shakespeare finds it necessary occasionally to stick in asides for Edgar, to remind the audience this isn't really a madman, I'm just faking it.

Edgar's inconsistencies are hardly credible; this is expressionist drama. He has devised a whole role, in fact, for himself as Tom o'Bedlam, with a previous career. He tells the others out in the storm, I have been

> a servingman, proud in heart and mind; that curl'd my hair, wore gloves in my cap;

—that's what a young lover might do, wear the glove of his lady in his cap—

> serv'd the lust of my mistress' heart, and did the act of darkness with her; swore as many oaths as I spake words, and broke them in the sweet face of heaven; one that slept in the contriving of lust, and waked to do it. Wine loved I deeply, dice dearly; and in woman out-paramour'd the Turk. False of heart, light of ear, bloody of hand; hog in sloth, fox in stealth, wolf in greediness, dog in madness, lion in prey.

Hog, fox, wolf, dog, lion. Add them all up, what do you get? A man, but a very interesting kind of man. There's a strange relationship between this servingman, who does the act of darkness with his mistress, and other characters in this play. There is another serving man, Oswald, the serving man of Goneril, totally loyal to her, as loyal to her as Kent is to Lear, and even dies for her. He's also arrogant; he's very arrogant toward Lear at Goneril's bidding. As for doing the acts of darkness with one's mistress, Edmund, in the latter part of the play, pays court to both Goneril and Regan. Regan suspects that he has actually slept with Goneril, that they have done the acts of darkness. Edgar, in realistic life, doesn't know about all that, doesn't know about Oswald, doesn't know really what Edmund is doing. But that doesn't matter. Three is an obscure symbolic connection here. It is as if Edgar, in his debasement, must become the things that he eventually fights against. Oswald and Edmund are the two characters that Edgar kills before this play is over. Edgar kills Oswald in defense of Gloucester. He kills Edmund in defense of his own honor, in straightening out issues in the final scene. There's a formal medieval trial by combat. It is as if Edgar, who starts as an innocent dupe, must become those things that he overcomes, at the end of the play. Presumably, at the end of the play, he's going to be the next king of Britain. But first, he has become his enemies and sunk as low as he possibly could. It is as if we're having a surreal version of a story that Shakespeare has told already, the story of Prince Hal, becoming a wastrel, a madcap, a tavern drinker, a highway robber, before he can become a king. We get it in very compressed, very strange mirrored, oddly lit version.

Finally, I must talk about Lear, for Lear has a remarkable capacity to take in new experience, particularly if you consider his age, four score and upward. He does learn very fast; he does not go on making the same kind of mistakes as Macbeth does. For example, he has learned, before Act I is over, that he was totally wrong to treat Cordelia as he did. "I did her wrong," he says absolutely flatly. "It isn't even a small fault, after all." Angry as he is at his other daughters, at the ungrateful Goneril and Regan, he knows that there is more that he must do than simply curse them. I shall go to the end of Act II, to the climax of his second angry scene with these daughters, where they're trying to strip the train of knights from him. Those knights are, for him, the sole remaining sign of his former regal position. They keep saying, "Why do you need 100 knights?

Why do you need 50? Why do you need 25?" They pare him down all the way to nothing, that significant word for this opening movement of the play. Regan says, finally, at the end, "What need one?" Lear answers:

> O, reason not the need! Our basest beggars
>
> Are in the poorest thing superfluous.
>
> Allow not nature more than nature needs,
>
> Man's life is cheap as beast's.

If you argue everything in terms of absolute necessity, there is very little that we absolutely must have. We need food, we need shelter, we need some clothing. But there are all sorts of things we don't need. We don't need cars, we don't need cities, we don't need culture, civilization, we don't need tapes from the Teaching Company. We can survive scratching by on roots and berries. But somehow, cities, culture and tapes from the Teaching Company make things better, enrich our lives, make life more than a beast's life. But for true need, he goes on:

> You heavens, give me that patience, patience I need!
>
> You see me here, you gods, a poor old man,
>
> As full of grief as age; wretched in both!

He jumps from the physical needs and his desire to be treated with respect because of his former kingship, to a moral need. He realizes he needs patience, the ability to endure, the ability to suffer, the ability to grow morally. That is an important step forward.

It carries further in the storm scenes. His anger continues, and he enters Act III crying out to the storm, "Howl, winds." In fact, he's assisting the storm, urging it to blow even more harshly. But what I want to lay stress on is his growing concern for other people. There's a moment when he's left alone by Kent and the fool in the storm, when he prays. It's really Lear's only soliloquy, in Act III, Scene IV:

> Poor naked wretches, wheresoe'er you are,
>
> That bide the pelting of this pitiless storm,
>
> How shall your houseless heads and unfed sides,
>
> Your loop'd and window'd raggedness, defend you
>
> From seasons such as these? O, I have ta'en

> Too little care of this! Take physic, pomp;
> Expose thyself to feel what wretches feel,
> That thou mayst shake the superflux to them
> And show the heavens more just.

Being out in the storm, unhoused, unclothed, he realizes what many people have been through while he sat in a palace, on a throne, fed and comfortable. This is a plea for distributive justice, for the gods to make sure that everybody is aware of how everybody else suffers. It is his fault in Britain that the heavens have not been shown more just hitherto. He did not know how poor naked wretches felt. Note that he is not telling the heavens to arrange all this. It's "Take physic, pomp; / Expose thyself and show the heavens more just." The pompous people, the great people, must go and take physic, take medicine, expose themselves—that's the form the medicine takes—and it is their job to show the heavens more just. It is the job of the king of Britain to show that the heavens prevail justly in Britain. It is his fault that they haven't done so hitherto.

From that moral generalization about the fate of poor naked wretches, and the duty of other men, we get a very specific example. Just after that prayer, poor Tom o'Bedlam, Edgar in disguise, bounces out of the hovel, and he is the poor naked wretch, the embodiment of poor naked wretchdom. I talked about that disguise from Edgar's point of view and what it might symbolically represent in the subplot of the play. It is important also to talk about the disguise from Lear's point of view. What does he see when he looks on a poor naked wretch? For one thing, it drives him completely mad. He goes over the brink and is convinced that it must be unkind daughters who reduced this person to this condition. He's got this fixed idea, all disorder must come from unkind daughters. More important than that, he sees in poor Tom o'Bedlam the fundamental human condition.

> Is man no more than this? Consider him well. Thou owest the worm no silk, the beast no hide, the sheep no wool, the cat no perfume. Ha! Here's three on's are sophisticated! Thou art the thing itself; unaccommodated man is no more but such a poor, bare, forked animal as thou art. Off, off, you lendings! Come, unbutton here.

He begins to tear off his clothes. Edgar, poor Tom o'Bedlam, is unaccommodated man, the thing itself, the base root of mankind. Lear wants to join him in that naked, exposed state. He wants to learn from him. In fact, he goes on in the rest of the scene to call him a philosopher, to ask him what is the cause of thunder. He begins to sound like a pre-Socratic philosopher, asking very elementary but far-reaching questions about the nature of the universe. Here we have the roots of experience. Since he has not learned from being a king, perhaps he can learn from a beggar and a madman. You must go to the depths of experience before you find out what life really is.

Lecture Thirty-Three
King Lear: "Then We Go On"

Scope:

In this concluding lecture of the triptych on *King Lear*, we return to the theme of disintegration, but this time with the emphasis on integration—or perhaps better, re-integration—in the face of chaos. By the midpoint of the play, the characters have, to borrow a phrase from Beckett, fallen "far from help." The second half of *King Lear* offers some six possible ways to forge on in the face of adversity. As an unparalleled play of the human condition, *King Lear* provides us with the full panoply of situations, emotions, and lessons.

Outline

I. The second half of the play asks, with increasing intensity, how we can go on from chaos. Six ways appear to be suggested.

    A. One may attempt to reconstruct a just civilization through the formal process of a legal trial.

        1. Lear's attempted trial of Goneril and Regan (represented only by wooden household stools) in Act 3 Scene 6 becomes a mad parody of a nursery quarrel.

        2. The trial eventually asks the question *"unde malum?"*; that is, whence comes evil? Or why are people callous and cruel and do evil things? Various answers (e.g., the gods, inexorable dumb forces, the stars, etc.) are suggested in later scenes. Love and hate are presented as first causes.

    B. One may act charitably to others. Act IV is full of helping, acts of charity and forgiveness.

        1. Kent and Cordelia return to help Lear.

        2. Edgar helps his blinded father, Gloucester.

    C. One may kill oneself.

        1. Blind Gloucester attempts suicide from what he thinks is the Dover cliff in Act 4 Scene 6. This is the weirdest scene in Shakespeare. The Bard exploits the conventions of the bare Elizabethan stage to make this scene work.

        2. His despair is cured—by a combination of shock treatment and blatant deception.

D. One may rage defiantly against the world.

    1. Lear rages madly against "love," which he insists on portraying in terms of debased sexuality.

    2. He rages against "justice," which he insists on portraying as hypocrisy and tyranny.

    3. Lear rages against social injustice in Act 4 Scene 6.

    4. Lear reduces man to an animal who lusts and punishes—and weeps. The blind Gloucester's sobbing causes Lear to recognize and pity him and to preach patience on "this great stage of fools" just as a preacher might take the primal birth cry of humanity as his text.

E. One may come to self-recognition (*anagnorisis*): "I am a very foolish fond old man."

F. One may simply endure.

    1. Edgar suggests in Act 5 Scene 2 that endurance leads to ripeness. ("What? In ill thoughts again? Men must endure their going hence, even as their coming hither. Ripeness is all.")

    2. To this, Gloucester replies "And that's true, too," indicating that this is just one of many truths.

    3. All the older versions of the Lear story have both Lear and Cordelia surviving their travails and being restored in the end.

    4. Shakespeare's version is full of "false dawns"—good is done and justice partly vindicated, but the ending is tragic.

II. The last act suggests that there are more than six ways. It keeps producing more truths that must be endured.

A. What does Lear see on the lips of Cordelia just before he dies? This is the play's final mystery.

B. Like a distant sentry, Lear reports from the margins of our existence.

Essential Reading:

Shakespeare, *King Lear*.

Questions to Consider:

1. Count up the instances of *anagnorisis* in this play. To whom do they occur and where in the plot do they happen? How does this help to drive the action?

2. What does Shakespeare achieve by altering the conventional ending of the older Lear stories mentioned above? Is the ending fully satisfying or perhaps better, cathartic, in the Aristotelian sense?

Lecture Thirty-Three—Transcript
King Lear: "Then We Go On"

By the middle of *King Lear*, the characters have reached the condition of chaos, the condition where man is unaccommodated, where man is a bare, poor, forked animal. In order to talk about what happens thereafter, I will take a cue from a modern writer, Samuel Beckett, from his famous play *Waiting for Godot*. Late in *Waiting for Godot*, Vladimir asks Pozzo, "What do you do when you fall far from help?" Pozzo answers, "We wait until we can get up, and then we go on." That is what this lecture on *King Lear* is about; going on, what you do when you fall far from help. The action of the last part of *King Lear* explores at least six possibilities. I know that sounds like a lot; when I was taught outlining in grade school, I was taught never to have more than four subpoints, better yet three. But Shakespeare is an abundant writer, so six it will be.

One way to go on is to investigate human behavior in a formal trial, to attempt to impose justice upon human affairs. This play is, in fact, full of trial scenes. The opening love test is a kind of trial; Cornwall and Regan hold a kangaroo court on Gloucester before they blind him; at the end of the play, there is a formal medieval trial by combat, in which Edgar defeats Edmund. At least the right man wins there. The most interesting trial is the scene in the hovel, Act III, Scene VI, where Lear attempts to try Goneril and Regan for their offenses against him. Goneril and Regan are represented by two wooden stools, which he calls joint stools. It is a mad parody of justice. Serious accusations are made to sounds like nursery quarrels. "'Tis Goneril….I take my oath, she kicked the poor King her father.""Is your name Goneril?" "She cannot deny it." You bet she can't; it's a wooden stool. The trial turns out to be quite futile; it's the maddest of the mad scenes. But it does ask an important question. At one point in the trial, Lear as prosecutor says, "Let them anatomize Regan; see what breeds about her heart. Is there any cause in nature that makes these hard hearts?" That is, why are people callous and cruel? What is the cause of evil? A number of speeches later in the play can be taken as answers to that question.

What is the cause of hard hearts? Some say that the gods are malignant, as Gloucester does. "As flies to wanton boys are we to the gods. They kill us for their sport." Other say the gods are just, as when Albany says, "This shows you are above, / You justicers, that these our nether crimes / So speedily can venge!" Some say we are not the victims of conscious gods; we are merely the victims of inexorable forces, represented by the motions of the stars. Kent, commenting on the strange fact that the loving Cordelia was born of the same parents as the heartless Goneril and Regan, says, "It is the stars, / The stars above us, govern our conditions." Cordelia herself says there is no cause for hard hearts. When Lear says to her, "You have cause to hate me," she responds, "No cause, no cause." There are no causes for love or hatred. They are what philosophers call first causes. The issue—what is the cause and nature of these hard hearts—is never settled definitively. The question, what is the cause, is left to reverberate in our minds as we see the final actions of the play.

The second way of going on is to act charitably to others. Maybe Vladimir put the question wrong. Maybe the question isn't "What do you do when you fall far from help?" Maybe we aren't ever really far from help. In the fourth acts of *King Lear*, in particular, people are always popping up, and they do help one another. Way back in Act I, Kent had not obeyed the decree of banishment; he came back in disguise to serve his master Lear. Edgar does not respond to his father Gloucester's abuse of him with anger; in Act IV, he helps the blinded Gloucester. Cordelia returns from France to restore her father's sanity, to restore her father to the throne. Act IV is full of deeds of charity, deeds of love. It is, moreover, the sort of love that forgets all previous injuries. Neither Edgar nor Cordelia ever say a word in blame of Lear or Gloucester. They reveal no resentment whatever of the fathers who have done them wrong. Lear and Gloucester blame themselves; they come to fuller self-knowledge, but they are forgiven by those who love them with a forgiveness so complete that it does not need even to be uttered. It is just love that is acted upon. Unfortunately, love does not conquer all. Gloucester had helped Lear by sending him away to Dover when he found out that Regan and Cornwall had a plot on his life. For that, Gloucester is blinded. Cordelia helps Lear with an army; she loses the battle and is eventually hanged. Cornwall's servant, the nameless man who tried to save Gloucester's second eye, is fatally stabbed by Regan. Love has its effect, but the effect doesn't seem to have a long run.

So, there's a third way. What do you do when you fall far from help? Why put up with it at all? Why bear it at all? Why not just kill yourself? This way of going on is fully explored in the case of

Gloucester. His guilt and his suffering lead him to despair, so he asks mad Tom o'Bedlam to take him to Dover Cliff so he can jump off. About this scene, I'm going to go into some detail. It's the weirdest scene in Shakespeare. Edgar persuades the blind Gloucester that he is standing on the edge of a high cliff, 1000 feet. Actually, they're standing on flat ground; since Gloucester is blind, he doesn't know the difference. Gloucester falls forward, then Edgar, pretending to be another person down on the beach, helps him up and tells him he survived by a miracle. The gods have delivered him from his suicide attempt. By this combination of shock treatment and blatant deception, Edgar saves Gloucester. Edgar cures his father's despair.

On a realistic stage, a stage with a full setting, this wouldn't work at all. You can't believe that Gloucester would be so deceived. I don't think it works very well in the film or television versions of *King Lear*. There always has to be something, sand or grass, on which the characters are standing, that reminds you this is a real place, and it doesn't seem credible. But on a non-realistic stage, on the original Elizabethan stage, where there was no setting, and the characters were standing on bare boards all the way through the play, with no scenery, a stage where the audience's imagination is made to work to supply whatever scenery may be necessary, it is believable. We believe it because Shakespeare is exploiting the conventions of his own theater to make us believe it. While the characters are supposedly still standing on the top of Dover Cliff, Edgar has a long speech describing that cliff, the dizzy height, the vegetation halfway down and the tiny details on the beach far below. It is a speech like any other piece of verbal scene painting in Shakespeare, like Lorenzo describing the moonlit garden outside Belmont at the end of *The Merchant of Venice*; we are made to imagine they are in a moonlit garden. Or like a scene in Richard II, which begins, "Barkloughly Castle call they this at hand?" You know it's Barkloughly Castle, and they're in front of the castle battlements for the rest of the scene.

In this scene, Edgar describes Dover Cliff; the audience supposes we're on the edge of Dover Cliff. We don't know what's going to happen next. They didn't know what's going to happen next. Particularly, they didn't know what was going to happen in this scene, because Shakespeare invented in this scene; it isn't in the sources for his play. A properly responsive Elizabethan audience would suppose they are on Dover Cliff, or they're watching a scene on Dover Cliff, so that when Gloucester falls forward and then is picked up and told he survived this 1000-foot fall, we are as confused in the audience as Gloucester is. We wonder what is going on here. We've been tricked as much as Gloucester, so that we're made to share his astonishment, and the effect is believable. It's a brilliant piece of stagecraft. Unfortunately, the scene also carries a frightful implication. It would appear that the only cure for suicidal misery is complete delusion. If you want to avoid killing yourself when you've found out how horrible the world really can be, then believe a lie. Believe that some imaginary gods have intervened, particularly on your behalf, and saved your life. If you are not very strong, like Lear—Lear is naturally defiant—if you are an ordinary man like Gloucester, you have to be fed some made-up religion. That is really very scary.

End of way three; I will go on to way four. I just mentioned that Lear was defiant, and that is our fourth way of going on—anger, rage against the world. Directly after Gloucester's leap, Lear re-enters for his final mad scene, bedecked with weeds, entirely returned to nature, as it were, and in that form he rages against love and justice as he sees them now. Let me clear the ground just a bit. The original love test in this play was an offense against both love and justice. It was an offense against love because it tried to measure love. "Tell me how much you love me." It was an offense against justice because Lear tried to distribute the kingdom on the basis of this crazy measuring of love. The two subjects, love and justice, keep recurring as we go through the play. This is one of their big mad spins. Lear begins to talk about love, but love is reduced to sex, and sex is particularly unattractive.

> What was thy cause? Adultery?
> Thou shalt not die: die for adultery! No:
> The wren goes to't, and the small gilded fly
> Does lecher in my sight.
> Let copulation thrive; for Gloucester's bastard son
> Was kinder to his father than my daughters
> Got 'tween the lawful sheets.
> To't, luxury, pell-mell! …

—luxury means lechery in Shakespeare's time—

> Behold yond simp'ring dame,

—he has an hallucination of a court lady—

> Whose face between her forks presageth snow,
> That minces virtue, and does shake the head
> To hear of pleasure's name.
> The fitchew, nor the soiled horse, goes to't
> With a more riotous appetite.

This supposedly virtuous court lady, who has all the proper manners, is actually very self-indulgent in sex.

> Down from the waist they are Centaurs,
> Though women all above.
> But to the girdle do the gods inherit,
> Beneath is all the fiend's.
> There's hell, there's darkness, there's the sulphurous pit.

Sex is bestial, it's filthy, and it's disgusting. If I were to start talking about the details of that speech, you would find it quite astonishingly obscene. That's love. Then he goes on and has another speech, imagining justice, imagining a trial going on:

> See how yond judge rails upon yond simple thief. Hark in thine ear…. Handy-dandy, which is the justice, which is the thief? Thou hast seen a farmer's dog bark at a beggar? And the creature run from the cur? There thou mightst behold the great image of authority: a dog's obeyed in office.

Then he imagines he sees a policeman whipping a whore.

Thou rascal beadle, hold thy bloody hand!

Why dost thou lash that whore? Strip thine own back.

Thou hotly lust'st to use her in that kind

For which thou whip'st her. The usurer hangs the cozener.

The usurper, the big con man, the banker, the businessman, hangs the cozener, the little con man, the guy who sells the false gold watch on the street corner. It is people in power, people who have enough money, who arrange the laws to suit themselves, arrange the laws to punish the little thieves.

Through tatter'd clothes small vices do appear;

Robes and furr'd gowns hide all. Plate sin with gold,

The strong lance of justice hurtless breaks;

Arm it in rags, a pygmy's straw does pierce it.

I think these two speeches taken together—the mad speech about love being a kind of bestial sex, and justice being a mindless tyranny of those who have enough power to impose it—these two speeches amount to a definition of mankind, a thumbnail description, at least, of mankind. Aristotle said that man is the rational animal. Jonathan Swift modified it; he said that man is the animal capable of reason. He was a little less optimistic. Lear is saying here that man is the animal that lusts and punishes. Those are our defining activities, to lust after one another, to lust after one another, and to lash one another.

Man does one more thing. He weeps. Lear is delivering all these speeches in a mad scene where he's not sure of who he's talking to, but the other people on the stage are Edgar, dressed as Tom o'Bedlam, and the blinded Gloucester. There is a kind of breakthrough at this point. He seems to recognize Gloucester. Gloucester is down on his knees at this point, and he starts audibly sobbing. At that sobbing, Lear looks at him, and gets down there with him:

If thou wilt weep my fortunes, take my eyes.

I know thee well enough; thy name is Gloucester.

Thou must be patient. We came crying hither;

> Thou know'st, the first time that we smell the air,
>
> We wawl and cry.

That's our defining action. The first thing we do when we are born, we utter that terrible scream of an infant first tasting the air. That's our reaction to the world. Lear takes that as a text and sees himself as a preacher. "I will preach to thee. Mark. …. When we are born, we come to this great stage of fools." What an extraordinary image for him to adopt at that point, for a character on a stage to say, "When we are born, we cry—we cry because we are come to this great stage of fools" to remind us that we are in a theater watching him. It is as if Shakespeare took the back of the theater auditorium and lifted it up so we all slid onto the stage, along with the blind man and the madman. This is our human condition.

End of way four. What do you do after that? There's always the possibility that you will stop being mad, that you will be restored to sanity, that you will recognize something of yourself. That is what happens when Cordelia returns, bringing a doctor and healing her father. Her father, after sleep, music, fresh clothing and medicines, natural medicines, comes to some degree of recognition, that *anagnorisis* that I have been saying is one of the most important elements in Shakespearean tragedy, that we've seen in other Shakespearean heroes. Hamlet, near the end of his play, is no longer "such a fellow crawling between earth and heaven." He takes to himself a specific identity. He says in Ophelia's graveyard, "This is I, Hamlet the Dane." I take upon myself my destiny as prince of Denmark, not generalized man, but man born to a certain circumstance with certain duties to carry out—prince of Denmark, Hamlet the Dane.

Othello loses his identity in lines I quoted in an earlier lecture. When Lodovico asks at the end of the play, "Where is this rash and most unfortunate man?" Othello responds, "That's he that was Othello. Here I am," and the remaining moments of the play are his endeavoring to find out what "I" is left for him, what identity there is. That lies in the act of killing the Turk, being the defender of civilization against the forces of barbarism that lie outside the empire and within, within Othello himself.

For Lear, it is the line uttered to Cordelia. "I am a very foolish, fond old man, four score and upward." I'm not a king, I'm not a justice,

I'm not a lover, I'm not a father, I'm just a very old man, and a foolish one. Does that do any good? Yes, it does. He's reunited to his one loving daughter, Cordelia, who tenderly cares for him. His self-recognition leads to his recognition of her. For then, he goes on and says, "Do not laugh at me, / For as I am a man, I think this lady / To be my child Cordelia." They are restored to each other, and that is the most important thing for both of them, that they are together, and they love one another. Does it do any good in the long run? Well, unfortunately no. They go on and they lose the battle.

So, what is the sixth way to go on? Simply, to go on, to endure. This has to do with the whole shape of the story. The great difference between Shakespeare's play of *King Lear* and all the earlier versions of this old story is that, in the earlier versions, Lear and his beloved daughter Cordelia survive. They are restored to power and restored to each other. It's an ending out of romance but, in Shakespeare, they lose the battle and they die. Although he writes a tragic ending, Shakespeare keeps many elements that seem to predict a happy one. As the critic Gene Howard has observed, the play is full of "false dawns." Edgar becomes a hero, a knight in shining armor, kills his villainous brother Edmund in the duel at the end. Goneril and Regan, the wicked sisters, quarrel over Edmund, and Goneril poisons Regan. Cornwall is already dead, killed by that nameless heroic servant. Albany, the other son-in-law, becomes a hero too, recognizes the villainy of his wife Goneril, can cope with it, whereon she kills herself. Edgar has already saved Gloucester from despair, and Lear is movingly reunited with Cordelia.

Yet all the hopes that we might have had for a final happy ending are dashed. They not only lose the battle, but Edmund's sentence upon the life of Cordelia gets carried out before it can be reversed. I take as an emblem of all such fresh disappointing discoveries, one moment in the second scene of the last act, a very short scene, where the battle happens offstage. Edgar leaves his father Gloucester onstage while he goes off to fight in the battle. The battle is condensed into simply offstage noises, and Edgar rushes back on to tell Gloucester, "King Lear hath lost, he and his daughter ta'en. Give me thy hand; come on!" But Gloucester doesn't want to go any further. "No farther, sir. A man may rot even here." Edgar tries to cheer him up once again. "What, in ill thoughts again? Men must endure / Their going hence, even as their coming hither; / Ripeness is all." Gloucester replies, "And that's true too."

When I started teaching *King Lear* many years ago, I believed that Edgar, in those lines, had come closest to summing up the meaning of the play. We must endure our coming hither, our birth, our birth when we wail and cry. We must endure our going hence, our death, whenever that happens to take place. We must endure the time between; this is the condition of life, we must submit to it. What we can hope for is some ripeness. Ripeness is all. It's like Hamlet's statement to Horatio, just before the final scene of his play, "The readiness is all." In Edgar's case it's a richer metaphor. Readiness is an abstract term; ripeness is a more luscious term, suggesting fullness, maturity, possibly even sturdiness, the accomplishment of a complete course. Ripeness is all; that is the all that answers the great echoing nothings of the first act of the play.

As I just said, I once believed that to be as close as we could come to the meaning of the whole play. Then, after some years of teaching, it occurred to me to look more closely at the next line, Gloucester's response. "And that's true too." An utterly flat little line. What Edgar has said is true; it's as true as any other generalization, as true as saying the gods are just, as true as saying that the gods are unjust, as true as saying that love and hatred are first causes, as true as saying that man weeps and punishes, as true as saying that there are six ways of going on. Come on, there are undoubtedly more than six.

In the organization of this lecture I am delivering, there is one lie, one large structural lie. My outline is too neat; it asserts that there are six ways of going on. Nothing is that easily solved. There are no such countable limits. Surely there are as many ways of going on as there are people who have tried to go on, who have tried to cope with the pain of life, with the slings and arrows of outrageous fortune. Worse things keep happening; we keep trying to cope. Worse things keep happening in *King Lear*; the characters keep trying to cope. Indeed, the characters keep trying to end the play. Kent, Albany, Edgar, the three surviving characters, keep trying to say things in the last 10 minutes of the play that will bring the curtain down, that will make it be over, that will end the story, bring the tragedy to an end. "Ripeness is all" is one of those things. Kent has some contributions. Albany says, "Our present business here is general woe," and doesn't want to say anything more. Stretched as they are, Lear himself goes further. He sees something else at the end, and says so in his final speech. Over the corpse of Cordelia, he looks upon her and says, "Look on her, look, her lips, / Look there, look there!" Then he dies.

What does Lear see? That is the final question mark, the final mystery of this play. Is it hope and love, or despair and the malice of the gods? On this point, many essays have been written, many passionate statements made. Critics, who are normally content to be learned, intelligent, and observant, tend to cast aside their academic robes and make professions of faith, or assertions of hopelessness. What does Lear see on Cordelia's lips? I don't know. Kent, Albany and Edgar don't know either. From our point of view, and from theirs, Lear is what Cordelia has called him earlier in the play, a *perdu*. The word is French; it means "a lost man." In particular military terminology, it means the sentry in the most exposed position, the one furthest out from the body of the army. He's called a *perdu* because, almost certainly, he is lost. He'll never get back. He sends us his messages, we get the signals, but we'll never know what the last thing he saw was, because he won't live to report on that. We depend upon him to patrol our farthest reach into threatening territory.

Lecture Thirty-Four
Macbeth: "Fair Is Foul"

Scope:

In the final three lectures of this series, we turn to *Macbeth*. We will see some of the themes discussed in the other three great tragedies (for example, the order of the universe, human political and social order, the nature of virtue and of good and evil). There are also questions of religious significance (for example, free will versus predestination) embedded in the play, as we would expect in the post-Reformation world in which Shakespeare worked.

Outline

I. *Macbeth* is a tragedy that can readily be understood as affirming an ultimately orderly and beneficent universe.

   A. Terrible deeds occur, but the protagonist is a bad man who is ultimately destroyed by better men, as his wife is tortured and driven to death by her own guilt. Their behavior appears to be unnatural both in the sense of being wicked and in the sense of being foreign to them. Evil is something alien and perverse.

      1. Lady Macbeth's distortion of her own nature is clear in her invocation to "murdering ministers" in Act 1 Scene 5.

      2. Macbeth indicates the terrible price he is willing to pay for his own comfort in his greeting to the witches in Act 4 Scene 1.

      3. Both of them declare their willingness to perform the extreme, Herod-like act of tyranny: the murder of children.

   B. The murder of Duncan, a sanctified king, is clearly marked as a hideous act, producing chaos in nature (a fierce storm, the cannibalism of the royal horses) and in the state until the proper order is restored when Duncan's son Malcolm wins the crown.

      1. Malcolm declares that his final victory manifests divine providence, "the grace of Grace." But Malcolm's own line will be replaced by the Stuarts, as Shakespeare and his audience well knew.

2. Macbeth's tyranny is counterbalanced by the excellent rule of the English king, Edward the Confessor, praised in Act 4 Scene 3.

II. This orthodox reading of *Macbeth*, although defensible, neglects features of the play that are less optimistic.

   A. The final description of the Macbeths as "this dead butcher and his fiendlike queen" is understandable but far from satisfactory.

   B. From the battle against rebels described in Act 1 to the final praise for Young Siward, Scotland is a land in which savage butchery regularly occurs and inspires praise and admiration.

   C. Macduff is the hero who replaces Macbeth as the loyal warrior fighting for his king, but Macduff is responsible for as much blood as Macbeth is, and not just on the battlefield—he is unintentionally responsible for the death of his own mother and his own children.

   D. Thus, the forces of virtue are, without realizing it, as destructive as Macbeth's. Echoes and parallels between the opening and closing of the play underline this.

   E. There is no marriage at the end.
      1. The sacred dynasties are male and mutilated by the end.
      2. The masculine virtues of courage and honor exemplified by the better men who defeat Macbeth lack continuity without the female principle of nurturance.

   F. Malcolm tries too hard to civilize and tame the force of tragedy, to "recuperate" these cruel and bloody events in a cruel and bloody country for some providential order.

III. Crucial to our understanding of the nature and governance of the universe in which *Macbeth* takes place is the question of free will.

   A. Does Macbeth choose to kill Duncan, or does the prophecy of the witches mean that he has no choice in the matter?

   B. On this issue, the play engages the chief theological dispute of Reformation Europe: the conflict between free will and predestination.

C. Who are the "weird sisters?"

    1. Are they, in effect, fates, and is their prediction for Macbeth a destiny he cannot escape?

    2. Or are they temptresses who do not and cannot overcome Macbeth's free will?

D. The possibility of predestined, immutable damnation—a possibility that Macbeth may embody in this play—was the most terrifying of all in the mind of Reformation Europe.

Essential Reading:

Shakespeare, *Macbeth*.

Supplementary Reading:

Bradley, *Shakespearean Tragedy*, lectures 9 and 10.

Hunter, *Shakespeare and the Mystery of God's Judgments*, chapter 7.

Questions to Consider:

1. *Macbeth* can be read on many levels. Consider it as a history play and compare it with Shakespeare's others in that genre. Can you find common themes in Shakespeare's handling of such topics as the nature of kingship, liege loyalty, and what we might call today "problems of succession?"

2. Why do you think Macbeth killed his honored guest? You can frame your answer in terms of the "free will versus predestination" argument adduced in the lecture or in any other context (e.g., his wife pushed him into it).

Macbeth is a tragedy that can be readily understood as affirming an ultimately beneficent universe. God's in His Heaven and, in the long run, things are all right in the world. The world is a place of order, created by love, sustained by love. Occasionally, the forces of elemental strife may invade it in the pattern I described when I was lecturing on *King Lear*; those forces of elemental strife even may reduce part of the world temporarily to chaos, but they will withdraw. The forces of order, the forces of love, will be restored.

Terrible deeds may occur; terrible deeds do occur in the play of *Macbeth*. But the leading character is a bad man, or a man who turns himself bad, and he is ultimately destroyed by better men. His wife is tortured and driven to death by her own guilt. Their behavior appears to be unnatural, both in the sense of being wicked, immoral, and in the sense of being foreign to them. They have to, as it were, force themselves to do things alien and perverse to human nature. This is very clear when Lady Macbeth first appears in the play.

She reads the letter from Macbeth, reporting the prophecy of the witches. She wishes to fulfill that prophecy, to achieve "the golden round, / Which fate and metaphysical aid doth seem / To have thee crown'd withal." In order to fulfill the prophecy, she prays to evil spirits. Their nature is not named; she calls them "murdering ministers." Their function is clearly to alter her human nature to make her capable of murder or assisting in murder. She soliloquizes:

> The raven himself is hoarse
>
> That croaks the fatal entrance of Duncan
>
> Under my battlements. Come, you spirits
>
> That tend on mortal thoughts, unsex me here
>
> And fill me from the crown to the toe top-full
>
> Of direst cruelty! Make thick my blood,
>
> Stop up the access and passage to remorse,
>
> That no compunctious visitings of nature
>
> Shake my fell purpose nor keep peace between
>
> The effect and it! Come to my woman's breasts,
>
> And take my milk for gall, you murdering ministers,

> Wherever in your sightless substances
>
> You wait on nature's mischief!

She is to be transformed, unsexed, her blood made thick, the passage to remorse stopped up. Above all, her natural milk, the milk of her breasts that would nurture another generation, the milk that makes possible the continuity of the human race, is to be made poisonous, to be turned to gall which is a kind of poison. In order to do wicked deeds, we have to make ourselves wicked.

Macbeth has a somewhat similar speech, when he goes to visit the witches the last time. The witches have been around their cauldron, and he comes in. "How now, you secret, black, and midnight hags?" Frightful way to greet anybody, I must say. Then he goes on:

> I conjure you, by that which you profess
>
> (Howe'er you come to know it) answer me:
>
> Though you untie the winds and let them fight
>
> Against the churches, though the yesty waves
>
> Confound and swallow navigation up,
>
> Though bladed corn be lodged and trees blown down,
>
> Though castles topple on their warders' heads,
>
> Though palaces and pyramids do slope
>
> Their heads to their foundations; though the treasure
>
> Of nature's germens tumble all together,
>
> Even till destruction sicken, answer me
>
> To what I ask you.

Look what he's willing to sacrifice for the sake of having peaceful nights. He will tear down churches. He will swallow navigation up— that is, commerce. He will have bladed corn lodged—that is, do away with agriculture. The castles of the lords, the palaces of the kings, indeed, all of nature itself, nature's germens tumble all together. Nature's germens are her seeds, the sources of all life, not just human life, as in Lady Macbeth's speech. He's willing to do away with the whole lot of it, so long as he has a peaceful night. The degree to which these people are willing to destroy, and destroy themselves, is remarkable.

It goes one further step. Both of them are willing to declare themselves ready for the extreme act of tyranny, the murder of children. Macbeth, in fact, orders the murder of Macduff's family and "all unfortunate souls / That trace him in his line," that is, Macduff's children. That is the one murder we see onstage, the murder of little Macduff, a small boy. Lady Macbeth has a terrible speech early on, when she is persuading her husband into the murder. She says he's sworn to do it; now he's being reluctant. "If I had given such an oath, I would do it." She says so in the most terrible way:

> I have given suck, and know
> How tender 'tis to love the babe that milks me:
> I would, while it was smiling in my face,
> Have pluck'd my nipple from his boneless gums
> And dash'd the brains out, had I so sworn as you
> Have done to this.

I would have destroyed my baby in the most intimate possible moment between mother and child, the moment of giving the baby nourishment at the breast. The murder of children, particularly one's own children, is the most terrible thing one can do in the Shakespearean universe, the ultimate mark of tyranny, the sign of King Herod—King Herod who murdered all the little boys in Bethlehem, the innocents, in an effort to murder the Christ child Himself. Herod is the archetypal tyrant of the medieval stage, still remembered in Shakespeare's time; he has Hamlet talk about "out-Heroding Herod on the stage," and the Macbeths take upon themselves the badge of Herod.

This is what they are willing to do, and the wickedness of this is extended throughout the whole play. It is clear that Duncan is a sanctified king. His murder is clearly marked as a hideous act. It has all sorts of reverberations through Scotland. There is one of those terrible Shakespearean storms the night of that murder. The horses, the royal horses of Duncan, break out of their stable during the storm, and "'Tis said they eat each other." This murder is so bad; it produces cannibalism amongst horses, which are vegetarian animals. All these things go on until the proper order is restored, when Duncan's son Malcolm regains the crown.

Malcolm regards regaining the crown as an act ordained by providence. He closes the play by saying the proper order is put back together again.

> What's more to do, …
>
> As calling home our exiled friends abroad …
>
> Producing forth the cruel ministers
>
> Of this dead butcher and his fiend-like queen …
>
> This, and what needful else
>
> That calls upon us, by the grace of Grace
>
> We will perform in measure, time, and place.
>
> So thanks to all at once and to each one,
>
> Whom we invite to see us crown'd at Scone.

The important thing is the grace of Grace. "By the grace of Grace, / We will perform all in measure, time and place." Measure, time and place are restored, and it is by the Grace Himself, God Himself. God has intervened, properly restored the order.

That this sort of thing should happen is previewed in the long scene in England, the scene in Act IV—which is the only extended passage in the play when we are not focusing upon Macbeth or upon his wife—the scene where Malcolm and Macduff meet and plan the overthrow of Macbeth and incidentally, in passing, praise the reign of good King Edward of England, who happens to be Edward the Confessor, the only English king admitted to the level of sainthood. Edward the Confessor has the power of relieving the disease of scrofula, known as the King's evil, because the King's touch could cure the disease. Malcolm says of this disease:

> 'Tis call'd the evil:
>
> A most miraculous work in this good king,
>
> Which often, since my here-remain in England,
>
> I have seen him do. How he solicits heaven,
>
> Himself best knows; but strangely-visited people,
>
> All swol'n and ulcerous, pitiful to the eye,
>
> The mere despair of surgery, he cures…
>
> With this strange virtue
>
> He hath a heavenly gift of prophecy,

> And sundry blessings hang about his throne
>
> That speak him full of grace.

This is how a king ought to be, curing the ills of his people, taking care of swellings and ulcers in the commonwealth as well as in individuals, curing the evil. I think it's no accident that scrofula is referred to in that general terminology, "the evil." This is the good king who cures evil. That is what kings ought to do. That is what Malcolm will do when he carries out his reign as king of Scotland, once they've got rid of Macbeth.

This is the orthodox reading of *The Tragedy of Macbeth*. There are many essays dealing with this matter in detail. The Macbeths do terrible things to others and to themselves; there is loss and there is waste; but the universe will eventually right itself; Duncan's line is restored in Malcolm. Macbeth's original loyal bravery on behalf of the crown is restored in Macduff, who becomes the king's hero, the king's right-hand man, defending the proper crown of Scotland at the end of the play as Macbeth had at the beginning of the play against the insurrection of the Thane of Cawdor.

Of all Shakespeare's major tragedies, assertions about ultimate providential order are most credible with this one. They are difficult to believe, at least for me, with *King Lear*. The characters of *King Lear* end up merely helpless before the final blows of disaster. *Hamlet*, I can believe it more easily; Hamlet himself believes in providence. I'm not absolutely sure whether the play believes it. It may not be a great restoration of Denmark to have its royal court littered with corpses and taken over by the son of the ancient enemy, Fortinbras of Norway. Branagh ended his film of *Hamlet* with Fortinbras' soldiers tearing down the statue of Hamlet's father, a rather shocking close. And *Othello*? I argued in an earlier lecture that Othello confronts complete loss; in fact, he believes he's damned and asks only that his story be properly told. But *Macbeth* seems to end with a full restoration. Even with *Macbeth*, we may have some doubts. The longer I go on reading, seeing, and talking about this play, the less certain I am of the total restoration. As an interpretation, it works well enough, if you concentrate on the careers of Macbeth and Lady Macbeth, and consider the surrounding circumstances as poetic invocations of the standard Elizabethan world picture. But there are doubts; there are things that bother me. I'm bothered even by that final speech of Malcolm.

Appealing to "the grace of Grace and measure, time and place" is fine. Describing the Macbeths as "this dead butcher and his fiend-like queen," that rather bothers me. We know too much about the Macbeths to be happy with that description. He was a butcher, but he was more than that, he was other things. As for her being fiend-like, how does Malcolm know anything about that? Moreover, this is an extremely violent society. The battle at the end kills young Siward, the son of the English hero, English ally. It is his first battle, and all his father does is say, "Had he his wounds before?" That is, was he wounded in front, or was he fleeing from the battle when he was killed? Doesn't care about whether his son was killed, it's just was he killed well. Did he behave honorably in the battle? That's a little hard-hearted for me.

Scotland is a land in which savage butchery regularly occurs. In fact, Scotland is a land where savage butchery earns praise and admiration. The opening battle, the battle against the rebels, is reported to King Duncan in the second scene of the play. We are told that Macbeth "unseamed" the rebel "from the nave to the chaps," that is, from tummy to chin. Duncan answers by saying, "O worthy gentlemen." You're a worthy gentleman if you stick a sword into somebody's gut and rip it up to his head. Terrific, great. That's how you get on. The difference in Macbeth, in Act II, is that he kills a man who's asleep instead of a man who's on a battlefield. There's just as much blood in both cases.

I have my doubts about Macduff too. Certainly he is the loyal warrior who replaces Macbeth as honorable right-hand man, as defender of the King. But there are disconcerting things about Macduff too. I became most full aware of them in a production I saw, done by the Royal Shakespeare Company, that is fortunately available in videotape still. This is a production done in the late 70s, with Ian McKellen in the title role, Judi Dench as Lady Macbeth, and an actor called Bob Kent as Macduff.

One of the extraordinary things he revealed about Macduff—he wasn't inventing things, he was just finding things that are there in the text—he moved the emphasis of the big scene in England, the scene where he discovers that his own family have been killed. Ross comes as a messenger from Scotland to say so. That happens very late in the scene; the first part of the scene has to do with his testing Malcolm, to see if Malcolm is indeed a worthy heir to the throne.

Malcolm, in fact, describes himself as being very lustful, very avaricious. He wishes to "pour the sweet milk of concord into hell" and do all sorts of things. He's testing Macduff; is this man really trying to get me onto the throne of Scotland, or is he some agent trying to bring me into Macbeth's power? They're both testing each other. When Malcolm goes on at great length about his wickedness, the virtuous Macduff responds by saying, "I can't support a candidate for the crown like that." He put all the emotional emphasis of the scene there, at his horror at this wimp of a prince, who was not only full of all these lusts, but thereby disgraced his family, blasphemed his breed:

> Thy royal father
>
> Was a most sainted king; the queen that bore thee,
>
> Oftener upon her knees than on her feet,
>
> Died every day she lived.

—your mother was a saint. She prayed, she mortified herself; she was a very good woman. "Fare thee well!" I'll have nothing to do with you. He put all that emphasis on living up to the family, so that when, 10 minutes later in the scene, Ross comes and says, "Macduff, your family was slaughtered, and you weren't there," Macduff could only collapse, realizing that he, too, had betrayed his family far worse. It made a superb emotional sequence, but it carried a terrible implication for the redemption of Scotland.

This Macduff, who replaces the original Macbeth as loyal Thane, is, however unintentionally, responsible for the death of his own wife, his own children. Later, we discover he's responsible for the death of his own mother. He was from his mother's womb untimely ripped. That wasn't his fault; he didn't choose that. But it is exactly the opposite of Lady Macbeth's fantasy about ripping the baby from her breast and dashing the brains out. It's equally destructive. It is no less bloody. Before the nineteenth century, mothers simply did not survive Cesarean delivery. It was a last step to save a baby's life when the mother was doomed anyway. What I'm saying is that the forces of Virtue, who rescue Scotland at the end of this play, are no less destructive than the Macbeths who tyrannize over Scotland at the beginning of the play.

They don't, of course, think so. As I say, Malcolm thinks he is behaving by the grace of Grace. But there are too many repetitions, too many echoes in the final scenes of the play of the earlier ones for us to be extraordinarily optimistic. Malcolm is hailed three times as king in the final scene of the play, exactly what had happened to Macbeth when he met the three witches. "Hail Macbeth, Thane of Glamis! Hail Macbeth, Thane of Cawdor! Hail Macbeth, that shalt be king hereafter!" The ending of the play turns out to replicate the opening, rather than to redeem it. The replication includes one other detail, the distribution of new titles. At the beginning, the Thane of Glamis became the Thane of Cawdor. In the second act, Malcolm became the Prince of Cumberland. At the end of the play, Malcolm announces that all the Thanes will step up now to a new title. "My Thanes and kinsmen, henceforth be earls, the first that ever were in Scotland." Now there's a change. By the way, it's historically accurate; Malcolm did import the title of earl to Scotland. The Scottish lords are to be Anglicized, scrubbed up, made up into Southrons. For Shakespeare writing the play in the reign of James I, the detail had a significance that it lacked in his source, Holinshed; Holinshed was writing in the reign of Elizabeth. Because, of course, by 1606, the date of this play, the Scots had moved south. James I was now King of England; he had been James VI of Scotland.

But there's another disturbing thing. Banquo's line of kings, to which James I belongs, the eventual inheritors, the Stuarts, is not Malcolm's line of kings. The play repeatedly tells us, and by a spectacular vision of a line of kings, that the Stuarts rule all Britain, which, of course, everybody in 1606 knew very well. But any student of dynasties is forced to remember that, at the end of *Macbeth*, at least one violent revolution is still awaiting Scotland, to get rid of the line of Malcolm and put on the line of the Stuarts. Malcolm's enthusiasm at the end of the play is understandable in its own terms, but the audience knows that the full closure he proclaims did not, in fact, take place. The victory of Malcolm at the end cannot be understood by the audience to redeem Scotland in anything like the full sense that the victory of Henry Tudor redeems England at the end of *Richard III*. Malcolm can't know that, but we do.

There's one further step to go in this. I just cited by comparison to Malcolm's closure of *Macbeth* Henry Tudor, Earl of Richmond's, closure of *Richard III*. Henry's closure is redemptive because it involves a marriage. Henry the Lancastrian will marry Elizabeth of York, and the warring lines of England will be united in the new house of Tudor, which was still on the throne in the person of

Elizabeth I when Shakespeare wrote *Richard III*. But *Macbeth* doesn't include any woman for Malcolm to marry. Its most prominent woman is a wife who unsexes herself and declares herself willing to rip babies from her breast. Its only other named woman, Lady Macduff, is herself immediately killed after the death of her own child, partly because of the flight of her husband. This is a play in which dynasty is invested with sacramental power, both the political dynasty that holds the crown and the domestic dynasty whose emotional importance is so strongly stressed in the case of the Macduff family. But the dynasties that we see are, oddly enough, all male, lacking the nurturing female power that gives dynasty its lasting ability, that makes dynasty possible. The Macbeths have no children, the Macduff children are killed, and even Mary Queen of Scots is left out of Banquo's line of kings. Scotland is a violent society of fathers and sons. Each of the dynasties loses a father or the son—Duncan; young Siward; Macduff's son; and Macbeth. The masculine virtues of courage and honor, which Scotland celebrates, inherently lack the possibility for continuity. Although a very bad man is eventually defeated by much better men, the Scotland of this play remains a destructive and terrifying world.

That's finally why I have difficulty with the providential reading for the end of *Macbeth*. To say that Malcolm and Macduff restore or redeem Scotland is to tame or to civilize the full tragic effect. Malcolm wants to claim the rhythm of historical romance, where all sorrows are finally recuperated, as the providential historians thought that the Wars of the Roses were recuperated by their production of the Tudor line. Malcolm wants to tame or to civilize tragedy, to say that there is a proper response to evil and misfortune, to say that there is redemption in the grace of Grace. But we know that the Stuarts lie far off in the future, and we have just heard Macbeth himself talk, not about the grace of Grace and redemption, but saying that life is just "tomorrow and tomorrow and tomorrow, creeping in this petty pace from day to day."

Perhaps tragedy cannot be thus tamed or civilized, not at the end, and maybe not even at the beginning, for there is one final problem about whether this world of Scotland in Shakespeare's play is subject to the order of God. That problem has to do with the status of the choices people make. The action of *Macbeth* depends on a prophecy. "All hail Macbeth, that shalt be king hereafter." What is the status of that prophecy? Do the witches know merely that Macbeth will be king, they simply happen to be aware of this future fact? Or, second possibility, are the witches tempting him into making himself king? That is, are they demonic creatures? Are they devils?

The witches could either be simply old women, who have had some commerce with Hell, or they could be real natives of Hell, coming up to tempt human beings to damn themselves. Do they know merely that he will be king, are they tempting him to make himself king, or—third possibility—do they know for certain that he will murder in order to become king? Are they saying, "This you will do"—they know not only the result, but the means, that Macbeth will commit mortal sin in order to gain the crown? That is, does Macbeth have any free will in the matter? Here's a prophecy, you'll be king; do you have any choice about it? The most terrifying possibility in this play is that he doesn't, that he may not. And it is the most terrifying possibility in the intellectual world of Shakespeare's time.

Shakespeare's time is the time of the Reformation, which gave birth to the Calvinist theory of predestination. God, from the very foundation of the world, knew exactly what every one of us would do. He extends grace to some of us, damnation to most of us; only He knows the choices, we don't. But they are immutable choices. They cannot be altered. The traditional Roman Catholic position laid more stress on free will; you have the options, your choices will be responded to by salvation or damnation. There was even an intermediate possibility that some theologians entertained, that you could sin and choose freely to sin. You could repent, but at some point your heart would become hardened, and the possibility of future grace would be denied you.

This is the sort of thing that theologians were debating all the time, and it was extremely important, but most people were extremely bewildered by the matter. How could you possible know? Are we predestined, or do my choices really make a difference? Do I get to choose salvation or damnation? Or can I go a certain distance down the road, and then there's a cutoff point? If so, how do I know when the cutoff point is reached? I'm making a joke out of it, but it was terrifying to many people. Are our choices free? Could Macbeth have done other than he does?

Lecture Thirty-Five
Macbeth: Musing on Murder

Scope:

In this lecture, we attempt to go inside of Macbeth's mind to hear him, as it were, contemplate his action and motives as he delivers a soliloquy or interior monologue. By using this technique, Shakespeare is able to develop numerous perspectives for his audience to consider as the play progresses.

Outline

I. Macbeth's soliloquy in Act 1 Scene 7 ("If it were done") is Shakespeare's fullest development of interior monologue.

    A. Soliloquies in Shakespeare's earlier plays tend to take the form of asides aimed straight at the audience; however, in the fully developed approach of the later plays, a man alone doesn't address the audience, but merely muses to himself. We happen to overhear him.

    B. Although Macbeth is a villain like Richard III and Edmund, he is not, like them, an ironist entertaining us with sardonic wit. Instead he is "rapt" in his own thoughts.

    C. He thinks associatively, not logically. He may not be fully conscious of the process by which he moves from one idea or emotion to another.

        1. Ian McKellan in playing Macbeth overrode the full stops and took his pauses in the middle of sentences.

        2. This is the most effective performance of this passage that the professor has seen.

II. Macbeth is at first reluctant directly to confront the idea of murdering Duncan.

    A. The soliloquy opens with an ambiguous generalization: is he making a moral or a pragmatic judgment?

    B. "Assassination" is an exotic and euphemistic word for murder.

    C. Macbeth does not refer to Duncan by name.

III. The phrase "bank and shoal [or school] of time" sets up three different contexts in which to evaluate the proposed murder.

    A. The first is risky physical action by a body of water.

    B. The next is teaching in a lecture hall (time is an arena wherein we learn lessons).

    C. Finally, there is passing judgment in a law court (time is a forum in which we are judged, perhaps for all eternity, a thought that Macbeth wishes to avoid).

IV. Macbeth's inner argument can be seen also in both secular and religious terms.

    A. Macbeth argues against murder in term of earthly sanctions (reasoning, in effect, that "what goes around, comes around").

    B. However, the words "chalice" and "host" suggest a religious, supernatural condemnation and punishment for murder.

    C. Macbeth also invokes the double, actually triple, trust in which King Duncan is held:

        1. He is Macbeth's king, kinsman, and guest.

        2. The sanctions are ultimately divine.

        3. There is a strong web of barely unconscious associations in Macbeth's thoughts here at this juncture.

V. The observation that Duncan's "virtues will plead like angels trumpet-tongued against the deep damnation of his taking-off" suggests a full scale Last Judgment.

    A. In Bernard of Clairvaux's allegory of the Four Daughters of God, the virtues that "plead" before God's throne are Justice, Truth, Mercy, and Peace.

    B. The ultimate result of their pleading was the birth of a Redeemer, Christ.

    C. The Redeemer will grow from baby to judge.

    D. Macbeth, in this amazing baroque passage, has vividly imaged forth a universal tempest of divine wrath that will be unleashed against him should he commit the enormity of murder, especially the murder of the Lord's anointed, who is also his guest and relative.

    E. Against this, Macbeth finds that only his vaulting human ambition spurs him on. He knows, perhaps somewhat inchoately, that his attempt to "jump" eternity is futile from the start. He is cut off amid this train of thought by the arrival of Lady Macbeth, who will prove to be the "spur" of his vaulting ambition.

F. By this abrupt close of this remarkable speech, we know more about Macbeth and what is going on in his mind than Macbeth himself consciously knows.

G. Macbeth may not fully understand all the implications of what he has said, but he has experienced their emotional effect.

Essential Reading:

Shakespeare, *Macbeth*.

Supplementary Reading:

The detailed notes on Macbeth's soliloquy in the Arden edition edited by Kenneth Muir or the New Cambridge edition edited by A. R. Braunmuller.

It is useful also to look up all the words used in this speech in the *Oxford English Dictionary* (complete version).

Questions to Consider:

1. Given all the arguments against murder that Macbeth comes up with in his soliloquy, why doesn't he—or can't he—talk himself out of the evil deed?

2. Can we instructively compare Macbeth to Hamlet in his introspection and hesitancy? If so, to whom or what can we compare Lady Macbeth?

Lecture Thirty-Five—Transcript
Macbeth: Musing on Murder

This lecture is about one speech only, the soliloquy that Macbeth utters at the beginning of Act I, Scene VII. It would be helpful to you in following it if you had a copy of the speech in front of you.

I have spoken about soliloquies before. Soliloquies in early Shakespeare tend to be a direct address to the audience. When Richard III comes out and tells us his plots, he is directly sharing those plots with us, inviting us to join in as silent co-conspirators. He hides no secrets from us; he knows everything he's going to say to us the moment he opens his mouth. As Shakespeare goes on in his career, his soliloquies become more interior. We get inside the man more. Hamlet still does some direct address, reasoning with us. But at times, we're really following Hamlet's reasoning—so that we get a feeling; and then we get him standing back and looking at that feeling, surprised to have heard himself say the things he's just said, taking different tracks, not having thought it out, but thinking it out just now.

With Macbeth, we reach the fullness of that process. Macbeth's soliloquy, "If it were done," is musing, is the interior life of a man who is not an extrovert, who does not go around exposing himself to all and sundry. He's a villain, like Richard III, but unlike Richard III, he's not an ironist, he's not an entertainer, he doesn't joke with us. He's alone with his thoughts. He muses. He is often rapt; that's a key word for him, used several times in the play, "Look how our partner's rapt." He's seized; he's enclosed in the thoughts, in the images of his own mind. The images of his own mind are extremely powerful. He has a notable imagination. We just happen to overhear him, by theatrical convention, as he pursues his thoughts, not knowing what he will think next. He doesn't know either; often he surprises himself.

He thinks associatively, not logically. He may not be fully conscious of the process by which you move from one idea, or one emotion, to the next, so that he comes out with things he doesn't intend to. The most effective portrayal of Macbeth's soliloquies that I've seen onstage has been from Ian McKellen. That performance is still available on videotape. McKellen had developed a kind of mannerism, a trick, of ignoring the period, the grammatical period, the full stop in the sentence, so that he would overrun the end of a sentence and take into the same breath the first words of the next sentence. Then he would pause and realize, "I've gotten into a different thought, where does that go?"—and then run forward, overrunning the next period.

Eventually this got to be a very annoying mannerism. It was like watching a dancer who's always on the offbeat. But in this case, for Macbeth, it was very effective. A man's mind and feelings outrun his conscious intention. This soliloquy makes a decision. He decides not to commit murder. It is important for us to ask, as we listen to it, "Why is he deciding not to commit murder? Is this a practical decision: that he can't get away with it? Or is it a moral decision: that murder is a bad thing to do?" Let us take it chunk by chunk.

> If it were done when 'tis done, then 'twere well
> It were done quickly.

The opening is a generalization, a proposition, as the beginnings of Shakespeare soliloquies often are. As Bassanio says, "So may the outward shows be least themselves," a generalization about appearance and reality. Or as Hamlet says, "To be or not to be? That is the question." Here, "If it were done when 'tis done, then 'twere well / It were done quickly." There's an odd pause even in this generalization. Should there be a comma at the end of the line? Is he saying, "If it were done when 'tis done, then 'twere well"? That is, if it is done, completed, finished, accomplished, no consequences, when 'tis done, in the sense of performed, then 'twere well, then it's okay—if I can get away with it, in other words.

Or is it a matter of deciding how to do it? Is it a fresh thought, "it were well it were done quickly," let's get it done right away? He seems to be hovering between two different thoughts. It's characteristic of Macbeth that he isn't quite sure what he's saying. It is also characteristic of Macbeth that there's something in the background, something perhaps in the unconscious, because the line is almost a quotation. "That thou doest, do quickly" was said on a very famous occasion. It was said by Jesus to Judas at the Last Supper. "One of you will betray me." "Is it I, Lord?" He says quietly to Judas, "That thou doest, do quickly." Go, get it over with, I can't bear the waiting. If that echo is alive in our minds, it's appropriate, for Macbeth is playing the Judas role to his king. He is about to betray his king.

The most important word in that opening, in that first line and a half, the most frequent word, is "it." It occurs four times. I think it's significant that Macbeth cannot name the thing he is talking about. He's keeping it at arm's length. He doesn't say murder, he doesn't say killing; he just says "it." Then he goes on and gets a little more specific.

> If the assassination
>
> Could trammel up the consequence, and catch
>
> With his surcease, success.

This is a little more specific. At least he's giving a noun to the action. It's assassination. But, in fact, that's a rather exotic term, a euphemism for killing. This is the first time the word "assassination" occurs in the written English language, according to the *Oxford English Dictionary*. It's an unusual word. It comes from the Arabic. There was a tribe whose name for themselves sounded to the Crusaders like "assassin". They were supposed to be particularly ferocious in attack, so in the European languages, the languages of the Crusaders who encountered this group of Arabs, the word "assassin" came to mean killer. The word "assassin" does begin to turn up fairly frequently in English in the sixteenth century, but it's only now, 1606, that is the beginning of the seventeenth century, that the full abstract form, assassination, gets written down. It's like referring to sexual intercourse not with a crude word beginning with F, but something like "coitus," or "sexual congress," a euphemism. Not touching it directly, handling it with tongs.

Likewise, "catch with his surcease, success." To talk of somebody being murdered as "his surcease" is, again, indirect, handling it with gloves. Notice he doesn't name Duncan, either; it's just "his." He's scared of this subject:

> That but this blow
>
> Might be the be-all and the end-all—

Finally, with the word "blow," we get a concrete noun. This is going to involve a stroke with a knife, a blow. He wants that to be the be-all and the end-all. He wants no bad consequences, no incriminating evidence, nothing.

—here,

But here, upon this bank and shoal of time,

We'ld jump the life to come."

To complete the sense of that first sentence, what he's saying is, "If we can get away with it, here on this bank of time, here in the world, here on Earth, then I'll forget about the life to come. I will not think about it in religious judgmental terms. I will not worry about what God thinks about it, as long as I can get away with it amongst men." That's the sense of the opening six lines of the speech. But there's an extraordinary emphasis here, "That but this blow / Might be the be-all and the end-all—here, / But here upon this bank and shoal of time." You'll notice there's a pause just before the end of the line. "Might be the be-all and the end-all—here."

It is very difficult for an actor to pause just before the last word of an iambic pentameter line; all the energy of the line rushes through to the end. Yet we've got a full stop there, and thus tremendous emphasis coming down on the word "here" which is doubled because the word "here" opens the next line. "Be-all and the end-all—here, / But here upon this bank and shoal of time." I'm going to think entirely in practical terms, Macbeth is saying. Think about the worldly consequences of the crime, and only that—the consequences in time, which is described as a bank and a shoal. That is, time is some kind of sea, lake, or river, and it has a bank beside it. We're going to stay on the bank and stay clear of the water. But that's kind of a difficult image. The moment you begin defining time, you have to define it in relation to something else. What do you define it in relation to? Obviously, eternity is the bank of time, and if you jump to the life to come, aren't you likely to get a bit wet if you go around jumping on the edge of a body of water? There may be some sense that Macbeth cannot do what he wants to do, that is, think if it only in earthly terms.

But that word "shoal" is also ambiguous. In the text, in the First Folio, which is the only early text of *Macbeth* that we have, it is spelled "schoole." It looks like school. In fact, it is ambiguous.

The Elizabethans spelled the word "shoal" and the word "school" the same way. They pronounced it differently. Burbage, in uttering this line, had to say either "shoal" or "school," but we don't know which he said. We don't know which Shakespeare meant; it could be "this bank and school of time," in which case time is a school, and the bank part is the lecture hall, those raised tiers that the students in a big lecture hall sit in. Time is a place where we learn lessons. Why? Because eventually we have to go out of the school and apply them in the world. As with the river image, time implies an opposite, eternity. Do you learn your lessons well? They will determine your fate elsewhere.

There's one possible other meaning for the bank here, and that is, "bank" can also be a judge's bench. It is the English word for a court, the court of the King's Bench. Time may be a courtroom, where we receive trial and sentence, which, of course, will govern where we spend eternity. I know you think I'm making all of this up; I have got three meanings going for this "bank and schoole/school/shoal of time," but I think all three are evident in Macbeth's mind as he proceeds, although not at the moment he says that phrase. They come out. "In these cases / We still have judgement here," he says. That certainly is the courtroom sense of the word "bank." In these cases, in these legal cases, we still have judgment here. We can get judged here; we don't need to worry about eternity. We may get judged here on earth for committing murder. "That we but teach / Bloody instructions"—there's the school image surfacing. If we commit murder, we're people teaching other people how to commit murder. Macbeth is facing the problem that Bolingbroke faced. If you depose a king, you prove that kings are deposable, and implicitly invite others to depose you. "We but teach / Bloody instructions, which being taught, return / To plague the inventor."

"This even-handed justice / Commends the ingredients of our poison'd chalice / To our own lips." Justice is even-handed. That image we still know, we are still familiar with. It is on the front of half the courthouses in America; Justice with her scales, weighing things. But Macbeth has slightly altered it. It isn't scales. Justice is a person who hands a chalice, a cup of wine, to somebody else, poisoned, and then receives it back. Or, if you hand poisoned wine to somebody, they may pass it back to you. What goes around, comes around. That is, he's afraid of the consequences of crime. If he commits murder, he himself will be judged, or he himself will be murdered, even in a practical sense, even here on earth. You start using poison, other people will start using poison too.

I've referred to this vessel of wine as a cup or a goblet, but that's not the word that Macbeth uses for it. He refers to it as a chalice, which is, of course, a kind of goblet, a very fancy kind of goblet. But for 2000 years of Western history—well, in Shakespeare's time, only 1600 years of Western history—it has been a very special kind of cup indeed. It's the cup used in the communion service, in the Eucharist. Apparently, in Macbeth's mind, he isn't entirely divorcing himself from religious sanctions about murder, from Christian considerations. It isn't wholly practical. But he tries to wrench himself back to the practical to the earthly, to the worldly.

> He's here in double trust:
>
> First, as I am his kinsman and his subject,
>
> Strong both against the deed; then, as his host,
>
> Who should against his murderer shut the door,
>
> Not bear the knife myself.

About those lines, I have several things to say. First, it's the clearest example of how Macbeth's associations run away with him. He's saying he's here in double trust, and then he names three things: kinsmen, subject, host. It's like the Monty Python joke about the Spanish Inquisition. "Fear is the great weapon of the Spanish Inquisition. Fear and terrible accuracy. Fear and accuracy are the two great weapons of the Spanish Inquisition." And so on and so on, and they multiply. Double trust turns out to be three things; his tongue runs away with him, his associations run away with him. But they do manage to remain fairly worldly. The kin connection is an earthly connection. We are supposed to be loyal to our kin. The subject connection—he's sworn obedience to Duncan, he owes him protection, he would be violating that bond of trust as well. Finally, as host, the relationship between host and guest is protected, is special, particularly in a primitive society like the Scotland of this play. Hospitality has a very high value because, of course, a host and a guest are enormously at each other's mercy. Therefore, in all primitive societies—it's all over Homer as well—the guest-host relationship is particularly sacred. These are "strong against the deed;" he "should against the murderer shut the door, not bear the knife myself." These are worldly arguments, but they are also ultimately religious arguments. The sanction for the kin tie, for the vow of the subject, and for the hospitality relationship is ultimately divine. For Macbeth to mention a host, three lines after mentioning a chalice, suggests very much that somewhere underneath his mind is the ceremony of the Eucharist.

It's reasonable enough for him to think of it. The scene is opened with a procession of servants going by with material for Duncan's supper. "Enter a sewer, and diverse servants with dishes and service … over the stage;" that is the plates, the crockery, the silverware, and presumably the goblets also. It may be just because he's seen some cups being passed by, passing by, that Macbeth comes up with this chalice image. But then, he has his own association for it. Chalice, host, this supper won't stay in its place just as a supper in Inverness, and well it shouldn't. After all, what supper is Duncan eating out there? Which of the many suppers in Duncan's life is he consuming just at the moment? His last one, of course. His last. Duncan, as an anointed king, is a representative of Christ in this society. I think this web of unconscious associations just gets too strong for Macbeth to keep down, to keep in his subconscious. It breaks out.

"Besides, this Duncan"—He's finally named the man; you have the feeling that the underthoughts are indeed breaking through.

> This Duncan
>
> Hath borne his faculties so meek, hath been
>
> So clear in his great office, that his virtues
>
> Will plead like angels trumpet-tongued against
>
> The deep damnation of his taking-off

That really is a rush of words, a gorgeous rush of words and a very powerful rush of words. He's finally named the thing that he is afraid of, damnation. There is a Biblical association for what he is doing. St. Paul had written in his letter to the Corinthians, in writing about the Eucharist, "Wherefore, whosoever shall eat this bread and drink this cup of the Lord unworthily, shall be guilty of the body and the blood of the Lord….For he that eateth and drinketh unworthily, eateth and drinketh damnation." That's the link in Macbeth's Christian culture, between the eating and the drinking, and the idea of damnation.

Killing Duncan will be a damnable deed, as well as a deed that's dangerous on earth. In fact, he's got even a larger context for it. At line 18, Duncan's virtues will "plead like angels, trumpet-tongued against this deep damnation." He's thinking of particular virtues.

There is a medieval allegory, invented by St. Bernard of Clairvaux, that in the beginning, when Adam and Eve fell in the garden, there was a debate took place in Heaven before the throne of God. The four daughters of God appeared before the throne and pleaded—that in the legal sense, made cases—to God. The four daughters of God are Justice, Truth, Mercy and Peace. Justice said, "Man must be punished. He has sinned, and you said that if he ate the apple, he would die." Truth supports Justice, and she adds, "It is indeed true that you said those things. It is indeed true that Adam and Eve have sinned. Therefore, they must die."

Mercy tries to intervene and say, "God, you are merciful, I am as much a daughter of God, that is, an attribute of God, as Justice and Truth are. You must extend mercy, or you will no longer be God." Peace joins Mercy, saying, "This is deplorable that there should be this argument in Heaven at all. Besides, if you don't grant mercy to man, there will be no peace between Heaven and earth." How is God to decide? Justice and Truth on the one hand, Mercy and Peace on the other. God must have all of them if he is to be God. The answer, of course, was the birth of Christ. Christ, by living and dying on the cross, takes the just penalty, fulfills the truth, and makes Mercy and Peace available to mankind.

This is a very familiar allegory for Shakespeare's time. It was the way the Middle Ages and the Renaissance dramatized a great problem; how could God be simultaneously just and merciful? The fact that God was both these things could be very nicely pictured on the wall of a church, by drawing God as an old man on a throne with the four daughters arguing before him, or dramatizing it in a play, which was done quite a number of times in the Middle Age and early Renaissance. Here, the virtues will plead like angels, but suddenly, the time frame of that pleading is accelerated. It becomes trumpet-tongued. It's moved from the beginning of things to the end of things, to the great trumpet, the end, to the Last Judgment, "against the deep damnation of his taking off."

"And pity, like a naked new-born babe"—Remember, the result of the debate of the four daughters was the birth of pity, Mercy, as a naked newborn babe, in the manger in Bethlehem.

> Pity, like a naked new-born babe,
> Striding the blast, or heaven's cherubim, horsed

Again, there's been a tremendous acceleration of the religious imagery. The Christ Child goes from being the baby to delivering the Last Judgment, coming down on the blast, becoming Michelangelo's terrible Christ, the Christ of the Last Judgment in the Sistine Chapel, hurling the sinners down to hell, in such a terrible way that even the Virgin turns aside from him, cannot bear the sight of all this damnation.

> Heaven's cherubim horsed
>
> Upon the sightless couriers of the air
>
> Shall blow the horrid deed in every eye,
>
> That tears shall drown the wind.

Those trumpets are still going. The trumpet tongues of the virtues, who are pleading like angels, come with the cherubim, come with the cherubim's horses, the sightless couriers of the air. They are blowing the horrid deed all over the world, creating tremendous storms and bringing the rain, the universal rain, of all mankind's tears at the horrible deed of murdering Duncan. Macbeth is surrounded by universal tempest, and it's all in condemnation of him. This is tremendous baroque imagery. It is like the painting of the ceiling of a baroque church, where you do have angels blowing trumpets in the corners, figures streaming across, and souls ascending and descending.

Macbeth has an extraordinary imagination. He doesn't seem to be able to argue out, in sober reason, the morality of the case. What he has is a vision of the morality of the case. He sees the wickedness of murdering Duncan as embodied in this vision of virtues, angels, and the last trump, the sightless couriers of the air, and this universal storm. He will be isolated. Storm, tears, wind, everyone consumed with horror at this deed—he himself is left alone. "I have no spur," in the final lines of the soliloquy,

> I have no spur
>
> To prick the sides of my intent, but only
>
> Vaulting ambition, which o'erleaps itself
>
> And falls on the other.

In comparison to that vast supernatural drama, with angels, angelic horses flying through the air, he is a mere mortal. He has no spur to prick the sides of his intent, except vaulting ambition. He's only got an ordinary earthly horse of normal flesh and blood. In fact, it's not even that. It's vaulting ambition, and he leaps on it, only to fall on the other side. It isn't even a living horse. It's that wooden thing down in the gymnasium, a vaulting horse. If you don't know how to use it, if you're not a properly trained gymnast, and you try to jump on it, you'll fall off on the other side. That's the futility of Macbeth's attempt to get away with murder. In comparison to the divine and human drama that will recoil upon him, he is merely jumping over a piece of wood, and not getting anywhere. The blow that started this speech, the blow that might be the be-all, turns into the blowing trumpets of damnation and condemnation. The jumping the life to come, his hope to escape any thought of condemnation in the Last Judgment, merely becomes an overleaping that falls on the other side.

The story of *Macbeth* is the story of a man who leapt in hope, but even as he did so, he knew he could not complete that leap successfully. In fact, he doesn't even complete the leap in this speech, because it ends without the full stop

> I have no spur
>
> To prick the sides of my intent, but only
>
> Vaulting ambition, which o'erleaps itself
>
> And falls on the other

Some editions add the word "side," supposing that it just got left out of the original text. I don't think that's what happened. What Shakespeare means is, Lady Macbeth comes in, and cuts him off. Here's the spur. Here's what's going to help him do this.

Macbeth has decided he will not do this. He has decided it—not clearly; I don't know whether he's conscious of everything I've just described as going on in these words. I'm sure that what's going on, I'm sure it's there. You can look up all the words in the *Oxford English Dictionary* and follow these trains of thought. But it is Macbeth's peculiar inner nature that he experiences it as a feeling, as a series of feelings and a set of associations. He couldn't sit down and diagram the argument. It is a wonderful exciting piece of writing to get inside a man's mind, and you know more about him than he consciously knows about himself.

Lecture Thirty-Six
Macbeth: "Enter Two Murderers"

Scope:

In this concluding lecture on *Macbeth* (and the concluding lecture of the series), we will continue the psychological probing begun in the last lecture. This time we will expand our scope to include Lady Macbeth, since her case is every bit as interesting, complex, and compelling as her husband's and perhaps even more so. We will explore the sexual undercurrents and overtones of their relationship, as well as look into the realm of "imagination" as we analyze this most searching of all of Shakespeare's portrayals of human self-destructiveness.

Outline

I. It is the unusual achievement of this play that we are brought into deep sympathy with two murderers while remaining fully aware of the horror of their crimes. The focus is on the Macbeths. Their victims appear in only a few scenes.

   A. This is not a modern story in which we can sympathize because the evildoers have themselves been mistreated prior to their crime.

      1. We are not given that kind of psychological motivation for them, and their crime is in fact unnecessary.

      2. If the weird sisters' prophecy is unconditional—at one point Macbeth thinks it is so—why does Macbeth have to do anything at all?

   B. They are not very able murderers.

      1. Lady Macbeth desires to kill, but cannot.

      2. Macbeth can kill in battle, but needs elaborate gearing up in order to kill Duncan (whose murder we don't actually see).

      3. Macbeth commits no further murders thereafter, but relies on hired thugs.

      4. Both Macbeths suffer enormous guilt over their act.

II. Only by a strange sexual cooperation can the Macbeths achieve their crime.

   A. Lady Macbeth imagines power and then suppresses her human and womanly faculties to act on her desire.

B. Macbeth is driven by imagination of the crime itself, yet his imagination is also "strong against the deed."

    1. In Act 1 Scene 3, he responds to the witches' prophecy by thinking of murder.

    2. In Act 2 Scene 1 (the "dagger" scene), he drives himself to the deed by imagining it as a theatrical scene. This imagining draws him on; he is emotionally both excited—and repelled—by these imaginings.

C. Lady Macbeth suppresses Macbeth's moral and pragmatic objections to the crime by making him think of the deed as manly.

    1. Here she knows she has a strong handle on her husband's emotions. She suggests that he would be a coward not to kill Duncan.

    2. Lady Macbeth's persuasion in Act 1 Scene 7 opposes males to females. Macbeth at first demurs, saying that too much aggression is not manly, but devilish.

D. Macbeth thus arrives at two motives aside from (and maybe overshadowing) his ambition:

    1. The imaginative appeal of the crime (the "glamour of evil").

    2. Lady Macbeth's appeal to his manliness.

III. *Macbeth* is Shakespeare's most searching portrayal of human self-destructiveness. We watch as Macbeth goes from a high pitch of emotion and imagination to a state of emotional and imaginative deadness after his crime.

A. He achieves no self-recognition; instead, he condemns life for its tedium and futility. As a dramatist, Shakespeare doesn't tell us whether this condemnation is right.

B. He loses his ability to respond emotionally to events.

C. Lady Macbeth undergoes a reverse process as the result of psychological self-mutilation.

    1. She starts out unimaginative and then becomes extremely imaginative, as (perhaps significantly) only in her sleep she is tortured by the sense of self-pollution that the crime has brought.

    2. She achieves a terrible self-recognition (*anagnorisis*).

Essential Reading:

Shakespeare, *Macbeth*.

Supplementary Reading:

Stephen Booth, *King Lear, Macbeth, Indefinition and Tragedy*.

Questions to Consider:

1. Who "wears the pants" in the Macbeth household? How does Lady Macbeth play on her husband's psychosexual makeup to overcome his objections to the murder of Duncan? Although we didn't do so in the course of the lectures, can you construct a Freudian interpretation of this play? A feminist critique?

2. Having now read and discussed them, can you say that one of Shakespeare's "big four" tragedies is his greatest play? Why or why not?

Lecture Thirty-Six—Transcript
Macbeth: "Enter Two Murderers"

"Enter two murderers"—that is a frequent stage direction in Shakespeare. The hired thugs of *Richard III*; there are murderers also hired in *Macbeth*; it occurs elsewhere in other plays. The great Shakespearean scholar Alfred Harbage, who was at Harvard in the middle of the century, once remarked that the whole play of *Macbeth* might be considered an expansion of the stage direction "Enter two murderers," taking it seriously; not just a couple of hired thugs, but the lead roles of the play. It is the unusual achievement of this play that we are brought into sympathy with two murderers. Shakespeare never allows us to forget the wickedness and horror of their crimes, but we see that wickedness as it tears apart the perpetrators, not the victims.

Except for the England scenes and the scenes that concentrate on Macduff and his family, we always are focusing upon the consciousness of Macbeth and his Lady. This is a striking theatrical and psychological move. It is, after all, easy to make touching the suffering of decent people who suffer abuse. Television shows that practically every night. It is rarer that we are shown the pain of wicked people, of people who know their deeds are wicked even as they commit them. Moreover, this is not the sort of story that has become popular in the twentieth century, where we sympathize with evildoers because we are made to understand the psychological origin of their wickedness. We are told the sad story of some youngsters who were badly brought up, who suffered abuse, who were subject to irresistible pressures. Therefore, their crimes are not only understandable, but also forgivable. That kind of explanation, that kind of easy sympathy, we are not given. We are not given that kind of background, that sort of early biography, for Macbeth and for Lady Macbeth. They are tempted, and they fall. That is it.

Their crime, in fact, is not the result of irresistible pressures insofar as we can humanly tell. The crime is, in fact, unnecessary. The prophecy that Macbeth has received from the witches is unconditional: you will be king. At least at one point, Macbeth recognizes it as unconditional; at one point, he dismisses the whole plan from his mind by saying, "If chance will have me king, then chance may crown me / Without my stir." I don't have to murder Duncan in order to get a crown for myself. After all, in this violent

Scotland in which they live, Duncan could be killed in the next war, or Malcolm could be killed. Duncan is old anyway. The crown seems to be elective amongst the royal family, and obviously Macbeth would be a leading contender whenever there was a vacancy of the crown. It could happen that Macbeth could become king without his committing any crimes to get there.

Further, Macbeth and Lady Macbeth do not seem to be extremely able murderers. This is not their natural, given thing. That may seem to be an odd sort of judgment; we don't normally evaluate people on whether they're able to commit murder or not. Indeed, the notion of Lady Macbeth doing the killing is considered rather shocking in the play. It is startling when she says of Duncan, "Had he not resembled / My father as he slept, I had done't." I think we're meant to think, "My God, I didn't even think that she might be up to sticking knives into people." That's not normally how women in this society behave. But Macbeth himself is not particularly able. He can kill in battle; he's very good at killing in battle, unseaming men from the knave to the chaps. But he has to gear himself up extraordinarily to kill in a castle, to kill a king in peacetime.

He takes no pleasure from it. He is haunted by guilt the moment he has done it. It is interesting how the murder is dramatized. We don't see the killing of Duncan; that takes place offstage. What we see is hundreds of lines whereby Macbeth prepares himself to do it, and then comes back onstage with the bloody daggers for more lines about his agonies, having done it. The concentration is altogether on the psychology of the murderer, and not on the suffering of the victim. He doesn't ever kill again. His subsequent murders, he does it secondhand. He hires thugs to kill Banquo and Fleance, to kill the Macduff family.

It is only by a strange cooperation between the two Macbeths that the murder of Duncan gets accomplished, a cooperation that is, in large part, sexual. The degree to which it strikes us as sexual in any given performance of *Macbeth* will depend, of course, on the casting of the leading characters, how much their sexuality reads, how much it is a sexual relation between them. But it's there in the language throughout. Lady Macbeth imagines power, she imagines "the golden round, / Which fate and metaphysical aid doth seem / To have thee crown'd withal." But she feels herself obliged to suppress her womanly faculties, her specifically sexual faculties, in order to assist

Macbeth to that end. I'd read, in an earlier lecture, the lines about "unsex me here, …Come to my woman's breasts, / And take my milk for gall." Unsex me so that I can be an adequate accessory to murder.

Macbeth is driven to the crime by his imagination. This is worked out in great detail. I want to pick up the play from the third scene of Act I, when Macbeth is given the prophecies. His response— "Macbeth, that are thane of Glamis, thane of Cawdor, Macbeth, that will be king hereafter"—his immediate response is a surprising one. He is silent; he is silent for a number of lines. Shakespeare points to the fact of his silence by having Banquo say, "Why do you start and seem to fear?" What's on your mind? It isn't for about 50 lines that Macbeth tells us what is actually on his mind. He has a long aside while Banquo talks to Ross and Angus.

> Two truths are told,
> As happy prologues to the swelling act
> Of the imperial theme…
> This supernatural soliciting
> Cannot be ill, cannot be good. If ill,
> Why hath it given me earnest of success,
> Commencing in a truth? I am thane of Cawdor.
> If good, why do I yield to that suggestion
> Whose horrid image doth unfix my hair
> And make my seated heart knock at my ribs,
> Against the use of nature? Present fears
> Are less than horrible imaginings:
> My thought, whose murder yet is but fantastical,
> Shakes so my single state of mind that function
> Is smother'd in surmise, and nothing is
> But what is not.

That, I suggest, is an extraordinary response to a prophecy that you will be king. He thinks not of a crown, purple robes, sitting on a throne, power, sleeping with anybody you like, and having ice cream every night. He thinks of murder. He's so intent on the idea of murder that it is more real to him then the thaneship of Cawdor, which he's just been told has been given to him. It is so real to him,

©1999 The Teaching Company Limited Partnership

that his hair stands on end, and that his heart pounds. He is rapt in that thought. This is our introduction to Macbeth's imagination, to the extraordinary degree of its power over him; how he is rapt in the images it produces. The fullest expression of this imaginative vision comes as he gears himself up for the murder itself, comes in the dagger soliloquy in the first scene of the second act.

> Is this a dagger that I see before me,
>
> The handle toward my hand? Come, let me clutch thee.
>
> I have thee not, and yet I see thee still.
>
> Art thou not, fatal vision, sensible
>
> To feeling as to sight?

I'll skip a few lines and go on.

> Now o'er the one half-world
>
> Nature seems dead, and wicked dreams abuse
>
> The curtain'd sleep; witchcraft celebrates
>
> Pale Hecate's offerings; and wither'd Murder,
>
> Alarum'd by his sentinel, the wolf,
>
> Whose howl's his watch, thus with his stealthy pace,
>
> With Tarquin's ravishing strides, towards his design
>
> Moves like a ghost. Thou sure and firm-set earth,
>
> Hear not my steps, which way they walk, for fear
>
> Thy very stones prate of my whereabout,
>
> And take the present horror from the time,
>
> Which now suits with it.

It is a very powerful speech indeed. Macbeth is imagining himself, visualizing himself, romanticizing himself. He is seeing himself as a figure in a dramatic scene. He is the murderer; this is how it should be. I am withered Murder—murder with a capital M—a personification. I am like Tarquin, the great Roman villain, and all the dramatic details have got to be right. The stones must not prate of my whereabouts, not because that would be a noise alarming the guests, waking the sleepers and preventing the murders from taking place, but because they're the wrong sound effect for murder. It would "take the present horror from the time."

The act of murder, to him, is in some way terrifically attractive. I don't mean he's a sadist—as I said earlier, he doesn't enjoy it. But somehow he's pulled to it; somehow he finds the commission of evil in itself attractive. He finds an emotional excitement, an exaltation, in the power a man has to murder. I can play this gigantic spectacular role; I can be Murder, causing a breach in nature, creating that vision of Duncan with "his silver skin laced with his golden blood." That imaginative desire, as much as any ambition, is part of Macbeth's motive. His imagination is, of course, also strong against the deed, as in the soliloquy that I analyzed in the last lecture. It is his imagination that produces visions of angels trumpet-tongued against the deep damnation of killing Duncan. His imagination, in other words, need reinforcement, needs a spur. His wife provides that by attacking him at his most vulnerable point, by attacking his manliness.

The first characteristic of Macbeth that had been impressed upon us in this play was his courage. He is an extraordinarily brave general, fighting against both a rebel and an invader, unseaming people from the nave to the chaps, "Bellona's bridegroom," brave Macbeth, who "doubly redoubles strokes upon the foe." It's a very bloody image, but because it's in the service of a king against invasion and rebellion, it's good. Macbeth is put in a position where this virtue of manly courage can exert a false appeal to him. He decides, in the soliloquy I last analyzed, not to murder Duncan. Then his wife comes in and tries to reverse his mind. He says, "We will proceed no further in this business." She immediately counter-attacks: "Was the hope drunk / Wherein you dress'd yourself?" Was this a weakness, something you'd say merely when you were drinking?

> Hath it slept since?
> And wakes it now, to look so green and pale

> At what it did so freely? From this time forth
>
> Such I account thy love.

That's even nastier than saying, "Were you drunk when you said you'd do this?" "Such I account thy love," you can't even command the respect of your wife any longer.

> Art thou afeard
>
> To be the same in thine own act and valour
>
> As thou art in desire? Wouldst thou have that
>
> Which thou esteem'st the ornament of life
>
> And live a coward in thine own esteem,
>
> Letting "I dare not" wait upon "I would"
>
> Like the poor cat i' the adage?

There she has said the terrible word, "coward." "Live a coward in your own esteem," you're going to have to think of yourself as a coward, never mind if I use the word. The reduction of a brave general to a domestic pet, "You're like the cat in the adage"—the cat that wouldn't get the food because it would have to get its paws wet. She's not arguing in moral terms at all. She's not talking about angels, trumpet-tongued and deep damnation and all that. She's going after him at a gut level. Are you man enough to do it?

He responds, "Prithee, peace! / I dare do all that may become a man; / Who dares do more is none." That's taking a moral stand on manliness. To do certain things are manly; to go beyond that, you would become a devil. But she takes it in other terms. She doesn't compare manliness to being a devil. She compares manliness to being a beast.

> What beast was't then
>
> That made you break this enterprise to me?
>
> When you durst do it, then you were a man,
>
> And, to be more than what you were, you would
>
> Be so much more the man.

Manliness doesn't consist of a moral standard. It consists of aggression, of courage, of machismo.

> Nor time nor place

Did then adhere, and yet you would make both.
They have made themselves, and that their fitness now
Does unmake you.

And then the terrible passage about giving suck.

I have given suck and know
How tender 'tis to love the babe that milks me:
I would, while it was smiling in my face,
Have pluck'd my nipple from his boneless gums,
And dash'd the brains out, had I so sworn as you
Have done to this.

I'm not going to talk about King Herod and killing babies anymore. I'm just going to go after the basic, gut, husband-and-wife relationship that's involved in saying such words. It means, "I'm a better man than you are; I'd stick to my word." That knocks Macbeth for a loop. He cannot repeat the arguments that had occurred to him in soliloquy; they don't seem to come back into his head about how immoral it is to kill Duncan, about the deep damnation of his taking off. All he can say is, "If we should fail?" What happens if it goes wrong? He's played into her hands at that point, because on that ground, on the ground of practicality, she can sweep everything before her.

We fail?
But screw your courage to the sticking-place
And we'll not fail.

An image taken, very appropriately, from an aggressive weapon, a crossbow: screw your courage to the sticking place, and then let fly the arrow. We'll not fail. She goes forth with the plans about how they'll do it, and he responds, "Bring forth men-children only; / For thy undaunted mettle should compose / Nothing but males." She is appropriate to bear only sons, not weak daughters. It is by persuading him that the murder of Duncan is a manly act, whereby he fulfills his manly capacity, that she gets him to do it.

Macbeth is then motivated by two things besides ambition: There is this deep attractiveness in killing, and there is also a fear of cowardice, a fear of being unmanly, that does away with the moral objections to murder. I think those two latter motivations are closely linked. You prove you are a man by murdering. That proves your grown-up, adult masculinity. That's why, I think, he invokes Tarquin in the dagger soliloquy, with Tarquin's murdering stride. Tarquin was not, in fact, famous as a murderer. That wasn't important about him. What was important about Tarquin was rape; he was a rapist. He raped Lucretia; Shakespeare wrote a long poem about it called *The Rape of Lucrece*. Rape, I think, is a primal male action. It is one of the few physical deeds that a man can perform, but a woman cannot. By invoking Tarquin in that way, he means to suggest—or he seems to think, he seems to be convinced, whether he's conscious of it or not—that murder is male. The ability to do a murder is a characteristic of a male. Lady Macbeth thinks so, too; the one moment she calls him husband is the moment when he comes back from killing Duncan with those bloody daggers in his hands. That's the point where she says, "My husband." It's a marvelous touch.

All of this is, of course, extremely perverse. It is the corruption of a noble quality, courage, by a complete disregard for its object, for the circumstances in which it is exerted. It is the corruption of manhood by too narrow a definition of manhood. It ruins Macbeth. It ruins his imagination, his most striking quality. Macbeth started this play with an imagination so vivid that he saw daggers in the air, and the very thought of a murder would make his scalp prickle in that way that makes us feel our hair is standing on end. At the end of the play, that imagination is dead. He is weary of everything; he has a desolating speech about his lack of response to any stimulus. He hears the cry of women, this terrible offstage shriek of the ladies in waiting of Lady Macbeth. He remarks on it:

> I have almost forgot the taste of fears:
>
> The time has been, my senses would have cool'd
>
> To hear a night-shriek,—

Just to hear a single cry in the middle of the night would have sent a chill down my spine—

> and my fell of hair
>
> Would at a dismal treatise rouse and stir
>
> As life were in't. I have supp'd full with horrors;
>
> Direness, familiar to my slaughterous thoughts,
>
> Cannot once start me.

Then his servant comes in and explains the cry of women; Lady Macbeth is dead, and all he can say about that is, you time it badly, dear. "You should have died hereafter."

Lady Macbeth goes through a parallel change, but it happens in reverse. At the beginning of the play, like her husband, she is exhilarated, rapt at the thought of the crime. Her exaltation comes about as the result of a deliberate act of will; she has asked evil spirits, the spirits that tend on mortal thoughts, to possess her. Unlike her husband, she has no ability to imagine consequences, no visions of angels trumpet-tongued. She energetically pushes Macbeth into the murder, making the practical plans by which it will be carried out. Her practicality in the murder scene itself is summed up in the line about the blood on their hands: "A little water clears us of this deed." Quite simple. The only thing that has to be done with blood is wash it off.

By the end of the play, she has developed an imagination, a rich inner life, a moral sensitivity. Her will is broken, and she releases that imagination in the anguish of her sleep. "A little water clears us of this deed" becomes the line in the sleepwalking scene, "All the perfumes of Arabia will not sweeten this little hand"—a gorgeous line. What marks the break, the change for both of them, is the appearance of the ghost of Banquo. Lady Macbeth, of course, does not see it, and tells Macbeth to be a man and resist whatever it is that is on his mind. He asserts himself as a man and banishes the image of Banquo, thus, as it were, strangling his own imagination, his own capacity to see morality in a visual form. Thereafter he sees no more images, except the deceiving ones called up by the witches.

She exhausts herself in the effort to make him command her, and she is exhausted, in fact, asleep ever after. We never see her awake again. He retains his manhood, the aggressive courage, that his wife has declared to be the essence of manhood, but in order to do it, he has killed almost all the rest of himself, a great deal of his emotional life. Indeed, at the end of that scene, the scene with the ghost, he sums up his life by saying,

> For mine own good
>
> All causes shall give way. I am in blood
>
> Stepp'd in so far that, should I wade no more,
>
> Returning were as tedious as go o'er.

I'm so far into blood, there's no point in going back. That would be as tedious as going forward and killing more people. That's an understandable remark. What strikes me as odd is the adjective he uses, tedious. If there's one thing that Macbeth's life has been up until this point, it's untedious. This is a man who unseams people from the nave to the chaps, sees daggers in the air, meets witches, becomes king, kills his own king. This has been an exciting life. But now, it is all dust and ashes for him.

One consequence of this narrowing of Macbeth, of his violent limitation of his faculties, is that there is no scene of self-recognition for him. We expect a tragic character to grow in perception as the play goes on. As the tragic hero becomes ever more fixed in his situation, his faculties, his understanding, his perception grows. I've laid stress on the self-recognition speeches of Lear, Hamlet and Othello. "I am a very foolish, fond old man," "I am Hamlet, the Dane." Macbeth has no such speech of *anagnorisis*. He does not recognize anything new. He does judge himself. He does not see himself. Instead, he judges the world, and he describes life around him.

> Tomorrow, and tomorrow, and tomorrow
>
> Creeps in this petty pace from day to day
>
> To the last syllable of recorded time;
>
> And all our yesterdays have lighted fools
>
> The way to dusty death. Out, out, brief candle!
>
> Life's but a walking shadow, a poor player
>
> That struts and frets his hour upon the stage
>
> And then is heard no more: it is a tale
>
> Told by an idiot, full of sound and fury,
>
> Signifying nothing.

Life is meaningless; time is merely one tick of the clock after another, men are fools, the sun is but a candle, showing us the way to the grave. In particular, we are actor-fools, and bad actors at that. We strut and fret in meaningless emotion. Moreover, an actor, remember, has no choice about what he will say or do. A pre-existing script determines his actions. He has no free will. He can perform with more or less grace, but he can't change any of the outcomes. Even worse, life is a tale told by an idiot, full of sound and fury. We haven't even got the vibrant existence of actors. We are merely characters in a tale, flecks of sputum on the drool of an idiot. The idiot who tells the tale is presumably God. God is a fool, dribbling out our histories.

Is he right? Many critics, prone to gloom, have been seduced by the commanding mastery of those lines into supposing that this is what Shakespeare thought of life at the time he write this play. Other critics have said, of course, this is a bad man. If you kill everyone around you, it ought not to surprise you to find out you live in a wasteland. We are better guided by Malcolm, in saying that the grace of Grace finally asserts the power of good men over bad men like Macbeth. I don't know that Shakespeare bothers to decide who is right. That's not his business. His business is to depict the process, the experience.

This play is Shakespeare's most searching portrayal of human self-destructiveness. The destroyers, Macbeth and Lady Macbeth, are ultimately self-destroyers, and Shakespeare not only sympathizes with victims and with bystanders, but also has the extraordinary range to sympathize with those who do themselves in, with the villains themselves.

Timeline

Major Events in Politics, the Theater, and Shakespeare's Life

(See the Chart of Shakespeare's Plays for probable dates of individual plays.)

1509–1547 .... Reign of Henry VIII. He presides over the English Reformation, severing England from the Church of Rome. He begets three children who survive him, one each by the first three of his six wives. Small troupes of players tour the country.

1547–1553 .... Reign of Henry's son Edward VI. *The Book of Common Prayer* establishes an English liturgy for the Church of England.

1553–1558 .... Reign of Henry's elder daughter, Mary I (Bloody Mary). A Catholic, she restores England to Roman obedience. She marries Philip of Spain but dies childless.

1558 .... Accession of Henry's younger daughter, Elizabeth I. In the first years of her reign, the Protestant (Anglican) church is re-established by the Act of Supremacy (Elizabeth declared to be "Supreme Governor of the Church in England") and the Act of Uniformity (church attendance required upon pain of fines). *The Book of Common Prayer* is revised and republished. English translations of the Bible become standard: the Bishop's Bible for church use and the Geneva Bible for private reading. William Cecil (later

Lord Burghley) serves as Elizabeth's chief secretary.

1560s..Theatrical companies named after their patron lords begin regularly playing at nonce sites in London, as well as touring the country and playing at Court when asked. A purpose-built theater called the Red Lion is built in the London suburb of Stepney (it appears not to have lasted long).

1564 ....William Shakespeare born in the market town of Stratford-upon-Avon, Warwickshire, son to glover John Shakespeare and his wife, Mary Arden Shakespeare.

1568 ....Elizabeth's cousin, Mary Queen of Scots, having misruled Scotland since 1561 and having been forced to abdicate in favor of her infant son James VI, flees to England. She is kept confined in various castles, but by letter repeatedly conspires with various English and continental Catholics to take Elizabeth's crown.

1569–1570 ....Elizabeth puts down northern rebellion in favor of Mary Queen of Scots. Pope Pius V proclaims Elizabeth excommunicated and deposed.

1570s..Two outdoor amphitheaters are built for playing in the northern outskirts of London, The Theatre and The Curtain. Over the next four decades some seven other large theaters are built in the northern outskirts and on the south bank of the Thames River, but usually only two or three are in operation at any given time. Two small indoor theaters within London are used by companies consisting of choirboys.

1577 ....Francis Drake sets sail around the world (returns and is knighted in 1580). Raphael Holinshed publishes the first edition of *Chronicles of England, Scotland, and Ireland.*

1579 ....Thomas North publishes his English version of Plutarch's *Lives,* the major source for Shakespeare's plays on Roman subjects.

1582 ....Shakespeare (aged 18) marries Anne Hathaway (aged 26).

1583 ....Susanna, Shakespeare's elder daughter, born. The Queen's Men are established with the celebrated comic actor Richard Tarlton. They become the leading company in London and on tour for the decade.

1585 ....Hamnet and Judith, Shakespeare's twin son and daughter, born. Failed attempt to establish an English colony at Roanoke.

Later 1580s.................................The Elizabethan drama becomes a significant literary as well as commercial activity with the plays of Christopher Marlowe, John Lyly, Thomas Kyd, and Robert Greene. Sometime at the end of this decade, Shakespeare starts acting and writing.

1587	Mary Queen of Scots beheaded for complicity in plots against Elizabeth. Second edition of Holinshed's *Chronicles*, a major source for Shakespeare's plays on English history and for *King Lear, Macbeth,* and *Cymbeline.*
1588	With the backing of Pope Sixtus V, Philip II of Spain sends the Spanish Armada against England. It is defeated and dispersed by English ships and English weather.
1590	Edmund Spenser published the first three books of *The Faerie Queene,* the great Elizabethan epic poem (remainder published in 1596).
1592	Earliest surviving reference to Shakespeare as an actor and playwright (a sneering allusion by Robert Greene, including a line parodied from *3 Henry VI*) and the earliest surviving account of a performance of a Shakespeare play (an enthusiastic description by Thomas Nashe of the audience's emotional response to *1 Henry VI*).
1593–1594	Marlowe killed in a tavern brawl. A severe outbreak of plague keeps the London theaters closed for some eighteen months. Theater companies are disrupted. Shakespeare turns to writing narrative poetry, publishing *Venus and Adonis* and *The Rape of Lucrece.* When the playhouses reopen, all playing in London is in the hands of two newly consolidated companies: the Lord Admiral's Men at the Rose, with Edward Alleyn as their leading actor and Marlowe's

plays in their repertoire, and the Lord Chamberlain's Men at the Theatre, with Richard Burbage as leading actor, Will Kemp as leading comic, and Shakespeare as chief playwright.

1596 .... Shakespeare secures the grant of a coat of arms for his father, giving the family the right to describe themselves as gentlemen, members of the gentry class. Shakespeare's son Hamnet dies at age eleven. Ben Jonson's career as a playwright begins. Robert Cecil becomes Secretary of State as his father, Burghley, moves toward retirement.

1597 .... Shakespeare buys New Place, a large house in Stratford. The owner of the Shoreditch land upon which the Theatre stands refuses to renew the lease and attempts to take over the building, which is owned by Richard Burbage and his brother. The Lord Chamberlain's Men play at the Curtain.

1599 .... The Lord Chamberlain's Men tear down the Theatre and use its timbers to build the Globe Theater on the south bank of the Thames. They play there until 1642.

1601 .... The earl of Essex, Elizabeth's last favorite, rebels against her and is executed. Shakespeare's father dies.

1603 ....Death of Elizabeth I, accession of James I (James VI of Scotland). In the subsequent reshuffling of Court patronage, the Lord Chamberlain's Men become the King's Men, by which name they are known for the rest of their career.

1604 ....James I concludes peace with Spain (England has been technically and often actually at war with Spain since the Armada). At the Hampton Court Conference, James commands a new English translation of the Bible.

1605 ....Francis Bacon publishes *The Advancement of Learning*. Gunpowder Plot to blow up the royal family, and parliament (Guy Fawkes being one of the conspirators) is discovered.

1606 ....Francis Beaumont and John Fletcher begin their career as playwrights.

1607 ....Captain John Smith settles Jamestown. Shakespeare's daughter Susanna marries John Hall, physician of Stratford.

1608 ....Shakespeare's mother dies. Shakespeare's granddaughter, Elizabeth Hall, born (dies 1670, his last surviving descendant).

1609 ....The King's Men, having taken over the indoor theater in the Blackfriars district formerly used by boy companies, use it for their winter performances, while continuing at the Globe in the summers. Several other small roofed theaters within London come into regular use in the following decades, eventually becoming more important than the large amphitheaters in the suburbs. Shakespeare's *Sonnets* published, apparently without his cooperation.

1611 ....The King James Version of the Bible is published, and gradually becomes the standard English translation.

1612 ....About this time Shakespeare retires to Stratford. He appears to have written several of his last plays in collaboration with Fletcher, who then takes over as principal playwright for the King's Men.

1613 ....The Globe theater burns down during a performance of Shakespeare's and Fletcher's *Henry VIII*. It is rebuilt and reopens the next year.

1616 ....Shakespeare's daughter Judith marries Thomas Quiney, a Stratford vintner. Shakespeare dies at Stratford. Ben Jonson publishes his poems and plays in folio format under the title of *Works,* the first time such lavish publication had been given to contemporary stage-plays in England.

1618 ....Thirty Years War starts in Europe.

1620 ....English Pilgrims settle on the coast of Massachusetts.

1623 ....Death of Anne Hathaway Shakespeare. Two of Shakespeare's fellow actors, John Hemings and Henry Condell, publish in folio format *Mr. William Shakespeare's*

Comedies, Histories, and Tragedies (now called by scholars the First Folio). The volume contains 36 plays, of which eighteen had previously been available in cheap quarto format, and 18 had been unpublished. Not included are some plays now thought to have been at least partly written by Shakespeare.

1625 ....Death of James I, accession of his son Charles I.

1642 ....Parliament passes an act forbidding all playacting in England and closing the theaters. The theater companies dissolve.

1649 ....Charles I is executed after losing a civil war to parliamentary forces led by the Puritan Oliver Cromwell and being tried for treason against his own people. The monarchy is abolished and England declared a Commonwealth.

1660 ....Within two years of Cromwell's death, the monarchy is restored in the person of Charles I's son, Charles II. Theater is once again allowed in England. By this time, all the playhouses established in the 1560–1642 period have been demolished or adapted to other purposes. Some of the plays of Shakespeare, Jonson, and Beaumont and Fletcher are revived in new theaters.

1700–1800 ....Shakespeare's plays continue in production, often in adapted versions suited to the changing tastes of the times. He comes to be regarded as the greatest of English playwrights; actors become famous for their performances in his major roles. The plays begin to receive scholarly editions and commentary.

Chart of Shakespeare's Plays

This chart suggests the general course of Shakespeare's career as a playwright by listing all his plays vertically according to genre and horizontally according to date of probable first performance. In many cases the dates given arise from limited evidence that scholars interpret in different ways.

Date	Comedies	Histories	Tragedies	Romances
1589-93	The Two Gentlemen of Verona The Comedy of Errors The Taming of the Shrew	Henry VI Part 1 Henry VI Part 2 Henry VI Part 3 Richard III	Titus Andronicus	
1594-96	Love's Labor's Lost A Midsummer Night's Dream	King John Richard II	Romeo and Juliet	
1596-98	The Merchant of Venice The Merry Wives of Windsor Much Ado about Nothing	Henry IV Part 1 Henry IV Part 2		
1599	As You Like It	Henry V	Julius Caesar	
1600			Hamlet	
1601	Twelfth Night			
1602			Troilus and Cressida	
1603	All's Well That Ends Well			
1604	Measure for Measure		Othello	
1605			King Lear	
1606			Macbeth	
1607			Antony and Cleopatra	Pericles
1608			Coriolanus	
1609			Timon of Athens	Cymbeline
1610				The Winter's Tale
1611-13		Henry VIII		The Tempest The Two Noble Kinsmen

Other plays in which Shakespeare appears to have had a hand include:

- *Edward III*, a history performed before 1595 and printed in 1596; some scenes probably by Shakespeare.

- *Love's Labor's Won*, a comedy by Shakespeare with this title is mentioned in a book published in 1598 and printed before 1603. No copy is now known. Possibly it is one of the comedies listed above with an alternative title.

- *Sir Thomas More*, a history surviving in manuscript, to which Shakespeare contributed some scenes, perhaps around 1604.

- *Cardenio*, apparently a collaboration with Fletcher based on Cervantes, performed around 1613, never printed, now lost.

Glossary

action: used in these lectures in three related but differing senses. (1) Any physical movement on stage: entrances, duels, kissing, falling to the ground, crossing the stage. (2) The collective ongoing movement of the play, including not only physical movement but also dialogue, display of emotion, etc.; the movement of the story as a whole. (3) What a play is "about," usually put in a summary phrase; the action of *Richard II* is the fall of a king, the action of *The Taming of the Shrew* is named in its title, the action of *King Lear* might be described as Lear's self-discovery.

amphitheatres: also called "public theaters," large polygonal buildings in the suburbs of London, the playing-spaces of theater companies starting in the 1560s (see **hall theatres**). The audience stood in an unroofed yard around a large stage projecting from one wall, or sat in three stories of galleries surrounding the yard. Performances took place in the afternoon by natural light. Elizabethan accounts refer to their capacity as 2,000 or 3,000 people. The foundations of two, the Rose and the Globe, have been recently discovered. A full-size replica of the Globe has been built near its original site on the south bank of the Thames and now produces Shakespeare and other Elizabethan playwrights from May to September.

anagnorisis: (Gk: "disclosure," "recognition") the sudden revelation of important information, such as the real identity of a disguised character. In discussion of tragedy, it has come to be used especially for the protagonist's recognition of his faults, or of his real nature and position.

anti-Stratfordian: a person who believes that the plays performed and printed as William Shakespeare's were written by someone else and passed off under Shakespeare's name in a conspiracy to protect the identity of the real author. Anti-Stratfordians have proposed many different candidates for the authorship, most frequently Francis Bacon, Christopher Marlowe, and the earl of Oxford.

catharsis: the purgation of emotions. Aristotle considered the aim of tragedy to be the purgation of the emotions of pity and fear. The precise meaning of his brief statement has been disputed.

chorus: in Greek drama, 12 or 15 characters stood aside (largely) from the action and commented on it in choral lyrics to which they danced. In Elizabethan drama, a chorus is one person, speaking as representative of the acting company, usually presenting a prologue, epilogue, and other extra-dramatic speeches to frame the action.

climax: a moment in a play or a scene in which emotional tension or interest is at its highest, usually marking a turn in events.

company: a group of actors working together to put on plays. The Lord Chamberlain's Men were a legally chartered company consisting of six or eight sharers (the senior members who put up the money, organized the productions, paid playwrights and others for their work, played the leading roles, and took whatever profits there were), hired men (who for wages played minor parts and worked as theater functionaries), and several boys (apprenticed to senior members, playing the roles of women and children). There were also Elizabethan companies consisting entirely of boys, managed by a schoolmaster, choirmaster, or other adult.

conflict: the struggle(s) with which a play is concerned, between the protagonist and forces opposing him. Opposition may be provided by another character (the antagonist), by the protagonist's own conflicting desires, or by outside forces such as society, fate, the gods.

convention: the tacit agreement between actors and audience that certain stage actions correspond to certain experiences that might be difficult to reproduce realistically. In the Elizabethan theater, entrance with a torch signified that the scene was taking place at night. The term can be extended to practices of play-writing, such as the "aside" that can be heard by the audience but not by other characters on stage, or ending the play with an epilogue that directly addresses the audience requesting their applause, or the pretense that disguise makes a person utterly unrecognizable.

denouement: the resolution of the plot, in which the complications are unraveled and solved. Given the many plot lines of most Elizabethan plays, the denouement can be quite an elaborate scene.

dramatic irony: the term "irony" refers in general to a phrase or situation in which there are two levels of experience that contrast with each other. A dramatic irony occurs when the audience knows more than the characters do about the identity, the intentions, or the situation of a character.

dramaturgy: the art of writing plays.

Elizabethan: the adjective describing any person or thing dating from the reign of Elizabeth I (1588–1603). The equivalent adjective for the reign of James I (1603–1625) is Jacobean, of Charles I (1625–1649), Caroline. Many scholars use "Elizabethan" as an omnibus term to cover things (especially the plays) of all three reigns.

flaw: a fault or failing in a character, usually having consequences in the plot. Some critics hold that a flaw in the protagonist (what Aristotle called "*harmartia*") is crucial to the structure of a tragedy; others find the theory less useful.

exposition: information about events happening offstage or prior to the action of the play.

foil: a character used to provide contrast that will set off the qualities of another character. Shakespeare frequently uses dissimilar characters put in similar situations as foils to each other. Prince Hal uses the metaphor of foil (a metal used as background setting for a jewel) when outlining his plan to let his past behavior highlight his future reformation (*1 Henry IV*, 1.2).

folio: a book format: a single sheet of printing paper is printed on each side with two blocks of type and then folded once, creating two double-sided leaves, four pages. A book composed of such folded sheets was a large and lavish form of publication, used chiefly for history, theology, and other prestigious matter. Ben Jonson's printing of his play in folio was considered unusual and hubristic, but it set an example followed by Hemings and Condell for their collected edition of Shakespeare's plays.

hall theaters: often called "private theaters," these were smaller, roofed-over performance spaces, illuminated by candles, with the whole audience seated, charging higher prices than the amphitheaters. Used by companies consisting wholly of boys until about 1609, when the King's Men began the custom of using hall theaters for winter performances. Other adult companies followed suit.

hamartia: Aristotle's term for "failure" or "error" applied to the protagonist of a tragedy. Sometimes erroneously termed "tragic flaw," this term really applies more to what the character does than to any inherent flaw. Acting out of overweening pride (i.e., out of hubris) is often an example of *hamartia*.

pace: the speed at which a scene is acted, sometimes deducible from the way it is written.

peripety: a sudden reversal of fortune.

property (prop): an object used in the action of a play; e.g., a sword, a crown.

protagonist: in Greek drama, the "first actor"; i.e., the actor who played the largest role. By extension, the term means the central character in any play. In this sense, the word is more useful than "hero," since it may without awkwardness refer to a woman (Rosalind is the protagonist of *As You Like It*) and it avoids the favorable moral connotations of "hero": many plays have villains, such as Richard III and Macbeth, as protagonists. Strictly speaking, there can be only one protagonist in a play, but usage varies on this.

Puritans: Radical Protestants, those who wished to carry the reformation of the Church of England further, purifying doctrine, ritual and church government of elements still left from Roman Catholicism.

quarto: a book format: a single sheet of printing paper is printed on each side with four blocks of type and then folded twice, creating four double-sided leaves, eight pages. Single plays were usually published in this inexpensive format and sold unbound, with the folded pages merely stitched or tacked together.

soliloquy: a speech spoken by an actor alone on the stage.

speech prefix: in a written playtext, the name appearing before a speech, indicating who is to speak the words.

stage direction: in a written playtext, a statement indicating an actor's movements: e.g., "Enter Lear," "Exit Queen," "he dies." Elizabethan plays are usually sparse in stage directions compared to the lengthy descriptions given by Shaw and O'Neill, but often the reader may notice implicit stage directions in the spoken lines. When

Cordelia says to Lear, "No, sir, you must not kneel," clearly Lear has at least begun to kneel down.

suburb: as now, a town or settlement immediately outside a city, in Shakespeare's case, London. The associations of the term are quite different from those of today: they could be regarded as places of vice. Since London itself was ruled fairly strictly by the Lord Mayor and Aldermen, the owners of taverns, brothels, and theaters found it convenient to locate their establishments in suburbs.

Biography of William Shakespeare

Biographical information about William Shakespeare is sketchy: we know that he was born in Stratford-upon-Avon in England and was baptized on April 26, 1564. Although we celebrate April 23 as his birthday, the exact date is not known. His parents, John and Mary Arden Shakespeare, were solid citizens of Stratford, his father a tanner and glover and a dealer in farm produce, as well as a holder of various local offices. Nicholas Rowe, in his 1709 biography of Shakespeare, reported that William attended a grammar school, the King's New School at Stratford-upon-Avon, where Latin works would have formed the basis of the curriculum. In November 1852, at age 18, Shakespeare married Anne Hathaway, who was eight years older than he was. Their first child, Susanna, was born in May of the following year, and three years later the couple had twins, Hamnet and Judith, in February 1585.

The first reference to Shakespeare as an actor and dramatist in London came in 1592, in a critical mention in a work by another playwright, Robert Greene, who called Shakespeare "an upstart crow." Between 1592 and 1594, plague forced theatres to suspend performances. By late 1594, when Shakespeare was listed as a member of Lord Chamberlain's company, there were several plays to his credit (see timeline). From 1594 to 1601, Shakespeare was successful as a dramatist and actor in Lord's Chamberlain's Men, and, in 1599, his family was granted rank as gentlemen and was granted its own heraldic coat of arms. William Shakespeare was a part-owner of the best-known Elizabethan theatre, the Globe, which was built in 1599. After Elizabeth I died and King James I ascended the throne in 1603, Shakespeare's company became the King's Men and enjoyed the king's patronage. In 1608, Shakespeare and his company signed a twenty-one-year lease for the Blackfriars Theatre.

Surviving records attest to Shakespeare as a substantial property owner in Stratford and in London. He suffered the deaths of his son Hamnet in 1596, his father in 1601, his brother Edmund in 1607, and his mother in 1608. He returned to Stratford to live in 1611 or 1612 and died there on April 23, 1616. The largest share of his estate went to his married daughter Susanna, and a dowry went to his recently wed daughter Judith; by law, a third of the estate went to his wife Anne, although there was little mention of her in his will.

During Shakespeare's lifetime, some of his plays and poems were published without his permission. The sonnets were published in 1609, apparently without Shakespeare's involvement. The first complete edition of the plays, the First Folio of 1623, was based on manuscript copies and on prompt-books used by actors in the plays, materials that were collected by Shakespeare's fellow actors John Heminges and Henry Condell. There are no known surviving manuscript copies of any Shakespearean plays.

Bibliography

Primary Texts

Primary reading on Shakespeare consists of the plays themselves, which are available in many modern editions. Since Shakespeare wrote 400 years ago, the present lecturer recommends a text with good explanatory footnotes.

Paperback series such as Signet, Bantam, and New Penguin offer a single play per volume with footnotes and introductions. Some also offer an account of Shakespeare's life, an account of stage history, and lists of supplementary reading. They are easily portable, and one need buy only the plays one wants.

One-volume complete works of Shakespeare offer the similar footnotes and introductions for all the plays, plus substantial prefatory material on Shakespeare and his times, documentary material, and fuller bibliographies.

Although such a large book is cumbersome, the lecturer recommends any of the following:

The Complete Works of Shakespeare, ed. David Bevington, 4th edition updated, Addison Wesley Longman, 1997. (Used by the lecturer)

The Riverside Shakespeare, ed. G. Blakemore Evans, Houghton Mifflin, second edition, 1997.

The Norton Shakespeare, based on the Oxford Edition, ed. Stephen Greenblatt, W. W. Norton & Co., 1997. (The most comfortable of the three to carry and read. Some of its textual innovations have been disputed. The general introduction is good; some of the introductions to individual plays are tendentiously political)

Serious study of an individual play benefits from the more substantialmulti-volume complete works of Shakespeare, of which there are three outstanding series:

The oldest is the *New Arden Shakespeare*, published by Methuen from 1952 to 1982. These volumes are gradually being replaced with a re-editing known as "Arden 3," published by Thomas Nelson and Sons.

Two newer series are the *Oxford Shakespeare* and the *New Cambridge Shakespeare*, which started appearing in the 1980s from the University Presses of Oxford and Cambridge, respectively, and are not yet complete. These three series, publishing one play per volume in both hardback and paper cover, offer comprehensive introductions and detailed notes referring to the most recent scholarship and interpretation. Below are listed the plays in this course, with the names of the Arden, Oxford, and Cambridge editors. When no editor is listed, that particular play has not yet been published in that series:

Hamlet—Jenkins (Arden, 1982). Hibbard (Oxford, 1987). Edwards (Cambridge,1985).

Henry IV Part 1—Humphreys (Arden, 1960). Bevington (Oxford, 1987). Weil (Cambridge, 1997).

Henry IV Part 2—Humphreys (Arden, 1966). Weis (Oxford, 1998). Melchiori, (Cambridge, 1989).

Henry V—Craik (Arden, 1995). Taylor (Oxford, 1984). Gurr (Cambridge, 1992).

Julius Caesar—Daniell (Arden, 1998). Humphreys (Oxford, 1984). Spevack (Cambridge, 1988).

King Lear—Foakes (Arden, 1997). Halio (Cambridge, 1992).

Macbeth—Muir (Arden, 1951). Brooke (Oxford, 1990). Braunmiller (Cambridge, 1997).

Measure for Measure—Lever (Arden, 1965). Bawcutt (Oxford, 1991). Gibbons (Cambridge, 1991).

The Merchant of Venice—Brown (Arden, 1955). Halio (Oxford, 1993). Mahood (Cambridge, 1987).

Othello—Honigmann (Arden, 1997). Sanders (Cambridge, 1984).

Richard II—Ure (Arden, 1956). Gurr (Cambridge, 1984).

Richard III—Hammond (Arden, 1981).

Romeo and Juliet—Gibbons (Arden, 1980). Evans (Cambridge, 1984).

The Taming of the Shrew—Morris (Arden, 1981). Oliver (Oxford, 1982). Thompson (Cambridge, 1984).

Troilus and Cressida—Bevington (Arden, 1998). Muir (Oxford (1982).

Twelfth Night—Lothian & Craik (Arden, 1975). Warren & Wells (Oxford, 1994). Donno (Cambridge, 1985).

The New Arden Shakespeare is also available as a one-volume complete Shakespeare without notes or introductions, for those who want a "clean" text, uncluttered by scholars.

Secondary Material

Adelman, "'This Is and Is Not Cressid': The Characterization of Cressida." *The (M)other Tongue: Essays in Feminist Psychoanalytic Interpretation*, ed. Shirley Nelson Garner et al. Ithaca: Cornell University Press, 1985.

Altick, Richard D. "Symphonic Imagery in Richard II." Publications of the Modern Language Association, 62 (1947), 339-365.

Andrews, John F., ed. *William Shakespeare: His World, His Work, His Influence*. New York: Scribner, 1985. Essays by 60 modern scholars summarizing available knowledge of the Elizabethan world (volume I), Shakespeare's works (volume II), and the subsequent history of interpretation, production, and adaptation of those works (volume III).

Barber, C.L. *Shakespeare's Festive Comedy*. Princeton: Princeton University Press, 1959. A major book on the form and significance of the comedies.

Barkan, Leonard. "The Theatrical Consistency of Richard II." *Shakespeare Quarterly*, 29 (1978), 5-19. Characteristic texture and effects of the play.

Bate, Jonathan. *The Genius of Shakespeare*. New York: Oxford University Press, 1998. The best recent general book on Shakespeare (much better than Harold Bloom's over-promoted volume or the biography by Park Honan), dealing with the life, the career, and the nature of his genius.

Beckerman, Bernard. *Shakespeare at the Globe*. New York: Macmillan, 1962. The structural patterns and theatrical effects of plays in Shakespeare's time.

Booth, Stephen. *King Lear, Macbeth, Indefinition and Tragedy*. New Haven: Yale University Press, 1983. Rich and supple readings of the plays, starting from the expectations we bring to tragedy.

Booth, Stephen. "On the Value of Hamlet." In Kastan's collection of Hamlet essays listed below. This distinguished essay deals with the apparent incoherences and changes of focus in the play.

Bradley, A.C. *Shakespearean Tragedy: Lectures on Hamlet, Othello, King Lear, Macbeth*. London: Macmillan, 1904. A classic book on these four plays.

The culmination of nineteenth-century criticism, this book was more influential than any other in determining notions of Shakespearean tragedy for the first half of the 20th century.

Briggs, Julia. *This Stage-Play World: English Literature and its Background, 1580-1625*. New York: Oxford University Press, 1983. A useful, brief account of the intellectual and social backgrounds of Shakespeare's age.

Bullough, Geoffrey. *Narrative and Dramatic Sources of Shakespeare*. 8v. London: Routledge & Kegan Paul and New York: Columbia University Press, 1957-1975. A magnificent resource reprinting all of the sources of Shakespeare's plays with discussion of the ways in which he used them.

Cavell, Stanley. *Disowning Knowledge in Six Plays of Shakespeare*. Cambridge: Cambridge University Press, 1987. Essays on *Othello* and *Hamlet*, and an especially detailed and sensitive analysis of *King Lear* by a philosopher who has specialized in problems of aesthetics and value.

Coghill, Nevill. "The Basis of Shakespearean Comedy." *Essays and Studies*, n.s. 3 (1950), 1-28. Reprinted in Anne Ridler, ed., *Shakespeare Criticism*, 1935-1960. London: Oxford University Press, 1963. Comic theory, with a detailed reading of *The Merchant of Venice*.

Coghill, Nevill. *Shakespeare's Professional Skills*. Cambridge: Cambridge University Press, 1964. Contains an excellent essay on *Troilus and Cressida*.

Cook, Ann Jennalie. *Making a Match: Courtship in Shakespeare and His Society*. Princeton, 1991. Authoritative handling of marriage laws and customsin Shakespeare's time, and how Shakespeare uses them.

Danby, John F. *Shakespeare's Doctrine of Nature: A Study of "King Lear."* London: Faber, 1948.

Danson, Lawrence. *The Harmonies of The Merchant of Venice.* New Haven: Yale University Press, 1978. Book-length discussion of the play.

Dollimore, Jonathan & Alan Sinfield, eds. *Political Shakespeare: New Essays in Cultural Materialism.* Ithaca: Cornell University Press, 1985. Essays by "new historicists" and "cultural materialists" who concentrate on the ways in which literary texts participate in the social and political struggles of the era in which they were produced and in the eras in which they have been consumed.

Dollimore, Jonathan. *Radical Tragedy.* Chicago: University of Chicago Press, 1984. This feisty social and political reinterpretation of Renaissance tragedy includes a striking essay on *King Lear*.

Drakakis, John, ed. *Alternative Shakespeares.* London: Methuen, 1985. Essays by British feminists, Marxists, deconstructionists and other post-structuralist critics contesting the traditional liberal-humanist Shakespeare.

Goldman, Michael. *Shakespeare and the Energies of Drama.* Princeton, 1972. Focuses on stage dynamics and audience responses. Very perceptive on *Hamlet*, *Henry V*, and *King Lear*.

Greenblatt, Stephen Jay. *Shakespearean Negotiations: The Circulation of Social Energy in Renaissance England.* Berkeley: University of California Press, 1988. Includes "Invisible Bullets," a famous recent essay reinterpreting the history plays in terms of contemporaneous issues of class and culture.

Gross, John. *Shylock: Four Hundred Years in the Life of a Legend.* London: Chatto & Windus, 1992

Gurr, Andrew. *The Shakespearean Stage, 1574-1642.* Cambridge University Press, 3rd. ed., 1992. A compendium of scholarly information concerning the playhouses, and performance circumstances of Shakespeare's time.

Hawkins, Sherman. "The Two Worlds of Shakespearean Comedy." *Shakespeare Studies, 3* (1968), 62-80. Characteristic structural patterns and their significance.

Heilman, Robert B. "The Taming Untamed, or, The Return of the Shrew." *Modern Language Quarterly, 27* (1966), 147-61. An effort to restore the farcical nature of the play.

Howard, Jean E. *Shakespeare's Art of Orchestration: Stage Technique and Audience Response.* Urbana: University of Illinois Press, 1984. An illuminating account of Shakespeare's dramatic techniques.

Hunter, Robert G. *Shakespeare and the Comedy of Forgiveness.* New York: Columbia University Press, 1965. Essays on the comedies that deal with sin and repentance.

Hunter, Robert G. *Shakespeare and the Mystery of God's Judgments.* Athens: University of Georgia Press, 1976. Issues of free will and damnation *in Richard III, Hamlet, Othello,* and *Macbeth.*

Hunter, Robert G. "Shakespeare's Comic Sense as it Strikes us Today: Falstaff and the Protestant Ethic," in David Bevington and Jay L. Halio, eds., *Shakespeare: Pattern of Excelling Nature*, Newark: University of Delaware Press, 1978.

Kahn, Coppelia. *Man's Estate: Masculine Identity in Shakespeare.* Berkeley: University of California Press, 1981. A psychological study of male self-definition in the plays.

Kahn, Coppelia. "The Taming of the Shrew: Shakespeare's Mirror of Marriage." *Modern Language Studies, 5* (1975), 88-102. Deplores the farcical treatment of women.

Kastan, David Scott, ed. *Critical Essays on Shakespeare's Hamlet.* New York: G. K. Hall, 1995. Outstanding essays on Hamlet written since 1965.

Kastan, David Scott. "Proud Majesty Made a Subject: Shakespeare and the Spectacle of Rule." *Shakespeare Quarterly*, 37 (1986), 459-75. A major article on the stage deposition of kings, especially Richard II.

Kernan, Alvin B. "The Henriad: Shakespeare's Major History Plays." In Kernan, ed., *Modern Shakespearean Criticism*, New York:

Harcourt, Brace, and World, 1970. Classic statement of the ruling themes of the Lancastrian tetralogy of history plays.

Kernan, Alvin B. "The Plays and the Playwrights," in *The Revels History of Drama in English*, ed. Clifford Leech & T.W. Craik. Volume III. London: Methuen, 1975.

Kirsch, Arthur. *The Passions of Shakespeare's Tragic Heroes*. Charlottesville: University Press of Virginia, 1990.

Kitto, H.D.F. *Form and Meaning in Drama*. London: Methuen, 1956. This book on Greek tragedy has a fine chapter on *Hamlet*.

Knight, G. Wilson. *The Wheel of Fire*. Oxford: Oxford University Press, 1930. Includes a famous essay on the "Othello music."

Leech, Clifford. *Tragedy*. London: Methuen, 1969. A useful brief account of efforts to define tragedy.

Leggatt, Alexander. *Shakespeare's Comedy of Love*. London: Methuen, 1974. A perceptive book on love and social behavior in Shakespeare.

Lewis, C.S. "Hamlet: The Prince or the Poem." This classic essay is reprinted, among other places, in the Kernan collection listed above.

Lindenberger, Herbert. *Historical Drama*. Chicago: University of Chicago Press, 1975.

Loehlin, James. *Henry V: Shakespeare in Performance*. New York: St. Martin's Press, 1996.

Mack, Maynard. *Everybody's Shakespeare*. Lincoln: University of Nebraska Press, 1993. A great scholar-teacher's essays on the tragedies, including an excerpt from his book *King Lear in Our Time* and his classic piece originally published as "The World of Hamlet."

McElroy, Bernard. *Shakespeare's Mature Tragedies*. Princeton: Princeton University Press, 1973.

Miola, Robert S. *Shakespeare's Rome*. Cambridge: Cambridge University Press, 1983.

Neely, Carol Thomas, "Women and Men in Othello." *The Woman's Part: Feminist Criticism of Shakespeare*, ed. Carolyn R. S. Lenz et al, Urbana: University of Illinois Press, 1980. Summary of major criticism on the play, leading to a helpful feminist reinterpretation.

Neill, Michael. *Issues of Death: Mortality and Identity in English Renaissance Tragedy*. Oxford: The Clarendon Press, 1997. A recent book on the big issues of tragedy, with fine sections on *Hamlet* and *Othello*.

Ornstein, Robert. *A Kingdom for a Stage: The Achievement of Shakespeare's History Plays*. Cambridge, Mass: Harvard University Press, 1972. A subtle and sensitive response to Shakespeare's history plays, with an eye on the serious ethical issues they raise.

Rabkin, Norman. *Shakespeare and the Problem of Meaning*. Chicago: University of Chicago Press, 1981. Includes sensitive accounts of the multiple meanings of *The Merchant of Venice* and *Henry V*.

Rabkin, Norman. "Troilus and Cressida: The Uses of the Double Plot." *Shakespeare Studies*, 1 (1965), 99-136.

Rose, Jacqueline. "Hamlet—the 'Mona Lisa' of Literature." In the Kastan collection listed above. A recent meditation on readings of the play.

Saccio, Peter. *Shakespeare's English Kings*. New York: Oxford University Press, 2nd ed., 2000. An account of the medieval history that Shakespeare modified in writing his history plays.

Saccio, Peter. "Shrewd and Kindly Farce." *Shakespeare Survey, 37* (1984), 33-40. A fuller statement of the argument in Lecture Six.

Schoenbaum, Samuel. *William Shakespeare: A Compact Documentary Life*. New York: Oxford University Press, rev. ed., 1987. The most reliable and sensible of the many available biographies of Shakespeare.

Shapiro James. *Shakespeare and the Jews*. New York: Columbia University Press, 1996. The fullest account of this difficult subject.

Sher, Antony. *The Year of the King*. New York: Limelight Editions, 1987. A distinguished actor's account of preparing and playing the role of *Richard III*.

Sterling, Brents. "'Or Else This Were a Savage Spectacle.'" *Shakespeare: Modern Essays in Criticism*, ed. Leonard Dean. New York: Oxford University Press, 1961. The use of ceremony in Julius Caesar.

Stevenson, David L. *The Achievement of Shakespeare's "Measure for Measure."* Ithaca: Cornell University Press, 1966.

Taylor, Gary. *Reinventing Shakespeare.* New York: Oxford University Press, 1989. A witty account of the ways in which Shakespeare was been reinterpreted by succeeding generations.

Tillyard, E.M.W. *The Elizabethan World Picture.* London: Chatto & Windus. 1943. How some people of the 16th century imagined their world to be organized.

Tillyard, E. M. W. *Shakespeare's History Plays.* London: Chatto & Windus, 1944. A classic study of the history plays, now widely disagreed with.

Williams, Penry. *The Later Tudors: England, 1547-1603.* Oxford: Oxford University Press, 1995. Currently the most useful introduction to the history of the period. Chapters 10-13, on the social order, religion, and family structure, are very relevant to readers of Shakespeare.

Wilson, J. Dover. *The Fortunes of Falstaff.* Cambridge: Cambridge University Press, 1964.

Wilson, J. Dover. *What Happens in Hamlet.* Cambridge: Cambridge University Press, 1935. A old study, still valuable for understanding the ghost.

Films and Videos:

If you want to see Shakespeare and do not live or travel near on of the Shakespeare theatre companies, there are many films and videos, some fairly faithful to Shakespeare's scripts, some heavily adapted (in English and other languages). A complete listing up to 1989 is available in Kenneth S. Rothwell and Annabelle Henkin Melzer, *Shakespeare on Screen* (New York and London: Neal-Schuman, 1990). Leading English-language versions are:

The Complete Plays done by BBC and Time-Life. All the plays, some good, some not so good, videotaped in the late 1970s and early 1980s. Not commonly available at local video rentals, but can be secured from Insight Media (1-800-233-9910) or Ambrose Video Publishing (1-800-526-4663). May be available at good public or university libraries.

Individual plays often available by catalog sales or at video rental stores:

1. Three directed by and starring Laurence Olivier:

Henry V (1944)
Hamlet (1948)
Richard III (1955)

Olivier also plays the title role in the 1965 filmed version of a National Theatre Production of *Othello*, directed by Stuart Burge, and Shylock in a 1974 TV video on Jonathan Miller's National Theatre Production of *The Merchant of Venice.*

2. Three directed by and starring Orson Welles:
Macbeth (1948)
Othello (1952)
Chimes at Midnight (1966), also called *Falstaff*; script put together from parts of *1 Henry IV, 2 Henry IV and Henry V.*

3. Three plays directed by and starring Kenneth Branagh:
Henry V (1989)
Much Ado About Nothing (1993)
Hamlet (1996: the complete text, four hours long)

4. Three plays directed by Francisco Zeffirelli:
The Taming of the Shrew (1966, starring Richard Burton and Elizabeth Taylor)
Romeo and Juliet (1968, starring Olivia Hussey and Leonard Whiting
Hamlet (1990, starring Mel Gibson, Glenn Close and Alan Bates)
5. Various directors:

A Midsummer Night's Dream (1935, a Hollywood black-and-white spectacular directed by Max Reinhart, with the young Mickey Rooney, James Cagney, Olivia de Havilland and others, with Mendelsohn pouring from the sound track; great fun)

Julius Caesar (1953, directed by Joseph Mankiewicz, with James Mason, John Gielgud, Marlon Brando)

Macbeth (1971, directed by Roman Polanski; remarkably bloody)

Macbeth (1979, Ian McClellan and Judi Dench, based on Trevor Nunn's 1976 RSC production; very good acting, but hard to find)

Richard III (1995, starring Ian McClellan, set in a Fascist Britain of the 1930s)

Othello (1995, Lawrence Fishburne, Kenneth Branagh)

Twelfth Night (1996, directed by Trevor Nunn, starring Imogen Stubbs, Nigel Hawthorne, Helena Bonham Carter, Ben Kingsley)

King Lear (1983, directed by Michael Elliott, starring Laurence Olivier, for Granada TV, 1983)

Romeo and Juliet (1996, directed by Baz Luhrmann, set in Verona Beach, Florida, and shot in MTV style, with Leonardo DeCaprio, Clair Danes)

Al Pacino's *Looking for Richard* (1996) is about the problems of producing *Richard III* for a modern audience. It contains scenes from Shakespeare's play.

Midsummer Night's Dream (1999; directed by Michael Hoffman, Italy/UK; set
in late Victorian Italy (he lovers ride bicycles), with suitable operatic music; a fairy world of special effects supervised by the lush figures of Michelle Pfeiffer and Rupert Everett and the charmingly bewildered Bottom of Kevin Kline.

Shakespeare in Love (1998, directed by John Madden, screenplay by Tom Stoppard, US/UK); multiple Oscar®-winning film; Tom Stoppard's dialogue is replete with outrageous anachronisms; the story is charming and the jokes are sly; the theatres, streets, and costumes are authentic; and the acting, especially that of Gwyneth Paltrow and Judi Dench, glows.